Streams of Mercy:
a meditative commentary on the Bible

Year 2

To Martha –
many blessings!

Ann Fontaine

by

Ann Fontaine

authorHOUSE™

1663 LIBERTY DRIVE, SUITE 200
BLOOMINGTON, INDIANA 47403
(800) 839-8640
WWW.AUTHORHOUSE.COM

First published by AuthorHouse 11/16/05

ISBN: 1-4208-9074-3 (sc)

Printed in the United States of America
Bloomington, Indiana

This book is printed on acid-free paper.

Bible citations from:
The New Revised Standard Version of the Bible, copyright © 1989 by
the Division of Christian Education of the National Council of the
Churches of Christ in the USA. Used by permission. All rights reserved.

Psalm citations from:
The Book of Common Prayer and Administration of the Sacraments
and Other Rites and Ceremonies of the Church
Together with The Psalter or Psalms of David
The Church Hymnal Corporation, NY 1986
"Come Thou Fount of Every Blessing" from:
The Hymnal 1982, text by Robert Robinson (1735-1790), Church
Pension Fund, Church Publishing Incorporated, New York, 1985.

Photography credits:
"Haystack Rock, Oregon," James H. Fontaine 1985 Cover
"Fence in the snow with tree," Ann Fontaine 2002. Advent
"Vireo nest," Ann Fontaine 2005. Christmas
"Comet," Wally Pacholka of Astropics 2004 used by permission.
Epiphany
"Old Bridge" Ann Fontaine 2004. Lent
"Apple Blossoms" Ann Fontaine 2005. Easter
"Rapids" Ann Fontaine 2005. Pentecost
"Chairs in Sunlight" Ann Fontaine 2005. Proper 16
"Yellowstone Falls" Ann Fontaine 2001. Back Cover
"Author" Brad Christensen 2005 About the Author

Trademarks:
The "Starbucks" name is a trademark of Starbucks Corporation.
Week of 5 Epiphany: Monday

Preface

How to use this book

There are several ways you might use this book.

The first is to use it as a daily meditation. Read a reflection each day and savor it as you go through your day. Listen to your heart and mind as you play with the ideas.

The second is to just dip in to wherever the page falls open— sort of reflection roulette.

A third is for those who read the Daily Office from the Episcopal Church Book of Common Prayer. This book, for the most part, follows the cycle of readings for Year 2 of the Daily Office— found in the back of the BCP.

The index of scripture passages in the back helps locate specific Bible citations for those who are preparing sermons or want a comment on that passage.

You are invited to invent your own way of reading *Streams of Mercy.*

If you would like to read more reflections, subscribe to the author's daily meditation list by sending a blank email to:

dailyoffice-subscribe@yahoogroups.com

Some Notes on the Church Year

The reflections in this book are arranged by the seasons of the church year.

Advent is the new year for the church and begins after Thanksgiving. Advent is a season of reflection and preparation for the birth of Christ at Christmas.

The twelve days of Christmas are a time of celebration but also foreshadow the work of Christ in the world.

Epiphany occurs on January 6 and is the celebration of the visitation of the Magi. It is symbolic of the Good News going out into the whole world

Ash Wednesday and Lent move due to the date of Easter which falls on the first Sunday after the full moon that occurs next after the vernal equinox. Lent is a time of meditation on our journey as followers of Christ including where we have fallen short. It is also symbolic of Jesus' 40-day fast in the wilderness. Sundays are not counted as part of Lent as they are always a celebration of the Resurrection.

Easter is the primary feast day of the church. It celebrates the triumph of life over death.

Pentecost begins between mid-May and the first part of June and continues until Advent. Pentecost (or the Propers) is also called ordinary time. It is the season of walking our life's path and living in the world as followers in the Way.

Contents

Advent

"Therefore encourage one another and build up each other, as indeed you are doing."
~1 Thessalonians 5:11

Words of love
Hands to hold
A touch of tenderness
A look of understanding
Paving blocks
for the journey.

Week of 1 Advent: Sunday

For this very reason, you must make every effort to support your faith with goodness, and goodness with knowledge, and knowledge with self-control, and self-control with endurance, and endurance with godliness, and godliness with mutual affection, and mutual affection with love.
~2 Peter 1:5-7

Faith and love,
the beginning and end
of instruction.
Goodness, knowledge, self-control,
endurance, godliness, mutual affection,
are just words without
faith and love.

Monday

You will do well to be attentive to this as to a lamp shining in a dark place, until the day dawns and the morning star rises in your hearts.
~2 Peter 1:19b

Nightmares of loneliness
and terror fade when
the morning star
lights the heart.

Tuesday

"A man had two sons; he went to the first and said, 'Son, go and work in the vineyard today.' He answered, 'I will not'; but later he changed his mind and went. The father went to the second and said the same; and he answered, 'I go, sir'; but he did not go. Which of the two did the will of his father?"
~Matthew 21:28b-31a

Dreams of deeds
will not weed the garden
or pick the grapes.
When hands are callused
and dirt is under the fingernails
we know
we have done the work.

Wednesday

So also our beloved brother Paul wrote to you according to the wisdom given him, speaking of this as he does in all his letters. There are some things in them hard to understand, which the ignorant and unstable twist to their own destruction, as they do the other scriptures.
~2 Peter 3:15b-16

Wringing the words
between mind-fears
Sentences twist and turn
into knots and nooses.

Thursday

O LORD, you are my portion and my cup;
  it is you who uphold my lot.
My boundaries enclose a pleasant land;
  indeed, I have a goodly heritage.
I will bless the LORD who gives me counsel;
  my heart teaches me, night after night.
~Psalm 16:5-7

The banquet table is set
with bread and wine
lands of discovery
provide for all
who would take the time to eat.

Friday

Gracious is the LORD and righteous;
    our God is full of compassion.
The LORD watches over the innocent;
I was brought very low, and he helped me.
Turn again to your rest, O my soul,
    for the LORD has treated you well.
For you have rescued my life from death,
    my eyes from tears, and my feet from stumbling.
I will walk in the presence of the LORD
    in the land of the living.
I believed, even when I said,
"I have been brought very low."
    In my distress I said, "No one can be trusted."
~Psalm 116:4-9

The rope of compassion
encircles the drowning
Pulling us back to shore
wrapping us in blankets of life.

Saturday

8

Weeping may spend the night,
   but joy comes in the morning.
~Psalm 30:6

Evening darkens,
grief knocks at my door
and moves in for the night.
With the dawn
I pack his bags
and busy myself in life.

"I am the Alpha and the Omega," says the Lord God, "who is and who was and who is to come, the Almighty."
~Revelation 1:8

Trailhead,
Trail,
and
Trail's-end
You are there in wilderness,
the journeys,
and homecomings
of my life.

Monday

And Amaziah said to Amos, "O seer, go, flee away to the land of Judah, earn your bread there, and prophesy there; but never again prophesy at Bethel, for it is the king's sanctuary, and it is a temple of the kingdom."
~Amos 7:12-13

Truth cannot be spoken
in a place that worships
principalities and power.

Tuesday

"They tie up heavy burdens, hard to bear, and lay them on the shoulders of others; but they themselves are unwilling to lift a finger to move them."
~Matthew 23:4

Power puts stones
on sagging shoulders.
Love lifts the load.

Wednesday

"For you tithe mint, dill, and cumin, and have neglected the weightier matters of the law: justice and mercy and faith."
~Matthew 23:23b

Junk food
does not nourish
even when
silver and fine china
set the table.

"To the one who conquers I will also give the morning star."
~ Revelation 2:28b

Before the edge of dawn
I see the promise
bright
shining
solitaire
in the dark beauty of night.

Friday

Wake up, and strengthen what remains and is on the point of death, for I have not found your works perfect in the sight of my God.
~Revelation 3:2

Call out the EMTs
Breathe life into the soul
Prepare bread and wine for the spirit
Intensive care is needed
when death is so near.

Saturday

"How can you believe when you accept glory from one another and do not seek the glory that comes from the one who alone is God?"
~John 5:44

Imitation jewels
and fool's gold
sparkle with false light
Blinding us to
Treasure.

Week of 3 Advent: Sunday

The LORD sustains them on their sickbed
    and ministers to them in their illness.
~Psalm 41:3

Nurse of souls
Hand of grace
tender care
upholding me
in the days of illness.

"I know your works; you are neither cold nor hot. I wish that you were either cold or hot. So, because you are lukewarm, and neither cold nor hot, I am about to spit you out of my mouth."
~Revelation 3:15-16

Ice and fire
Freeze and burn
Tepid sits in the cup
Tasteless.

Tuesday

The proud have smeared me with lies,
    but I will keep your commandments
    with my whole heart.
~Psalm 119:69

Confusion of lies
Catch us into the web
Stuck and flailing
in the spider's silk.

Wednesday

"And while they went to buy it, the bridegroom came, and those who were ready went with him into the wedding banquet; and the door was shut."
~Matthew 25:10

Last minute
shopping
leaves
the bridesmaids out in the cold.
What if they had
just gone in
empty handed?

Thursday

The word of the LORD came to Zechariah, saying: Thus says the LORD of hosts: Render true judgments, show kindness and mercy to one another; do not oppress the widow, the orphan, the alien, or the poor; and do not devise evil in your hearts against one another. But they refused to listen, and turned a stubborn shoulder, and stopped their ears in order not to hear. They made their hearts adamant in order not to hear the law and the words that the LORD of hosts had sent by his spirit through the former prophets. Therefore great wrath came from the LORD of hosts. Just as, when I called, they would not hear, so, when they called, I would not hear, says the LORD of hosts, and I scattered them with a whirlwind among all the nations that they had not known. Thus the land they left was desolate, so that no one went to and fro, and a pleasant land was made desolate.
~Zechariah 7:8-14

Widow, orphan, alien, poor
Canaries in the mine
Warnings of disaster
in the tunnels of life.

"Come, you that are blessed by my Father, inherit the kingdom prepared for you from the foundation of the world; for I was hungry and you gave me food, I was thirsty and you gave me something to drink, I was a stranger and you welcomed me, I was naked and you gave me clothing, I was sick and you took care of me, I was in prison and you visited me."
~Matthew 25:31-46

In small
often forgotten deeds
we become
daughters and sons
inheriting blessings
from the will of God.

Saturday

"But those who do what is true come to the light, so that it may be clearly seen that their deeds have been done in God."
~John 3:21

The true heart
seeks the light
as the compass needle
seeks true north.

"But the angel said to him, 'Do not be afraid,'"
~Luke 1:13a

Angels and fear---
Every encounter
comes with a terrifying choice.
How will I answer?

Monday

"He raises up the poor from the dust;
he lifts the needy from the ash heap,
to make them sit with princes
and inherit a seat of honor."
~1 Samuel 2:8a

Ragged souls are led
to chairs of gold
Cracked, callused fingers
hold silver chalices
when the Holy One holds a feast.

Tuesday

"... he has scattered the proud in the thoughts of their hearts."
~Luke 1:51b

Powerful and mighty horses
grazing fat on the green grass
Bolt and scatter
at the startling sight.

Wednesday

Fear came over all their neighbors, and all these things were talked about throughout the entire hill country of Judea.
~Luke 1:65

Old women
giving birth.
Speechless men
singing.
It is a fear-filled,
wonder-filled
time
when the Holy One
walks the earth.

Thursday

When John heard in prison what the Messiah was doing, he sent word by his disciples and said to him, "Are you the one who is to come, or are we to wait for another?"
~Matthew 11:2-3

Sitting in the prisons of life
Has it all been for nothing
Or did we make a difference?

Friday

On either side of the river is the tree of life with its twelve kinds of fruit, producing its fruit each month.
~Revelation 22:2b

Original Fruit of the Month Club!!
What a gift
each month a different fruit
All sweet and nourishing
I will look for the present
and meditate on the juiciness of life.

December 24

Christmas

... an angel of the L<small>ORD</small> appeared to him in a dream...
~Matthew 1:20b

May we all have dreams
of angels
bearing messages
from God
to us
May we also
carry the Christ child
to Bethlehem
Egypt
and home.

Christmas Eve

In days to come
    the mountain of the Lord's house
shall be established as the highest of the mountains,
    and shall be raised up above the hills.
Peoples shall stream to it,
    and many nations shall come and say:
"Come, let us go up to the mountain of the Lord,
    to the house of the God of Jacob;
that he may teach us his ways
    and that we may walk in his paths."
~Micah 4:1-2a

Sometimes we need a map
before we can begin to
find the mountain.

Christmas Day

Then Simeon blessed them and said to his mother Mary, "This child is destined for the falling and the rising of many in Israel, and to be a sign that will be opposed so that the inner thoughts of many will be revealed— and a sword will pierce your own soul too."
~Luke 2:34-35

Love---
and your soul will be
slashed to the heart.

Sunday

We remember today, O God, the slaughter of the holy innocents of Bethlehem by King Herod. Receive, we pray, into the arms of your mercy all innocent victims; and by your great might frustrate the designs of evil tyrants and establish your rule of justice, love, and peace; through Jesus Christ our LORD, who lives and reigns with you and the Holy Spirit, one God, for ever and ever. Amen.

~Book of Common Prayer, Collect of the Day

The health of the nations
reflects in the lives of its children
Herod lives
when one child dies of hunger.

December 28: Holy Innocents Day

... an angel of the LORD appeared to Joseph in a dream and said, "Get up, take the child and his mother, and flee to Egypt and remain there until I tell you; for Herod is about to search for the child, to destroy him."
~Matthew 2:13

If angels appeared
in our dreams
would we take
all the children
to Egypt?

December 29

Beloved, I pray that all may go well with you and that you may be in good health, just as it is well with your soul.
~3 John 2

Flames burn brightly
in containers of clay.

When Jesus saw him lying there and knew that he had been there a long time, he said to him, "Do you want to be made well?"
~John 5:6

Do you want to be made well?
Ah, that is the question isn't it?
Illness as identity
Can seem like a familiar friend.

December 31

...and you shall be called by a new name
    that the mouth of the L<small>ORD</small> will give.
~Isaiah 62:2b

On this new day
raise your name as a sail
to the Wind.

For no king has had a different
        beginning of existence;
there is for all one entrance into life,
        and one way out.
~Wisdom 7:5-6

From one door to the next
I walk through this house of life
Will I discover it to be a home?

Then he was afraid; he got up and fled for his life, and came to Beersheba, which belongs to Judah; he left his servant there.

But he himself went a day's journey into the wilderness, and came and sat down under a solitary broom tree. He asked that he might die: "It is enough; now, O LORD, take away my life, for I am no better than my ancestors." Then he lay down under the broom tree and fell asleep. Suddenly an angel touched him and said to him, "Get up and eat." He looked, and there at his head was a cake baked on hot stones, and a jar of water. He ate and drank, and lay down again. The angel of the LORD came a second time, touched him, and said, "Get up and eat, otherwise the journey will be too much for you." He got up, and ate and drank; then he went in the strength of that food forty days and forty nights to Horeb the mount of God.

~1Kings 19:3-8

When angels appear
with hot cakes and water
It may be a long journey.

"I alone am left, and they are seeking my life, to take it away." Then the LORD said to him, "Go, return on your way to the wilderness of Damascus; when you arrive, you shall anoint Hazael as king over Aram. Also you shall anoint Jehu son of Nimshi as king over Israel; and you shall anoint Elisha son of Shaphat of Abel-meholah as prophet in your place.... I will leave seven thousand in Israel....

~1Kings 19:14b-16, 18a

Terror blocks
ability to see
the thousands.

January 3

"Take no part in the unfruitful works of darkness, but instead expose them. For it is shameful even to mention what such people do secretly; but everything exposed by the light becomes visible, for everything that becomes visible is light."
~Ephesians 5:11-14

Stones turned over
reveal the ground
where nothing grows.
Light awakens the long dead seed.

January 4

The waters closed in over me;
    the deep surrounded me;
weeds were wrapped around my head
    at the roots of the mountains.
I went down to the land
    whose bars closed upon me forever;
yet you brought up my life from the Pit,
    O LORD my God.
~Jonah 2:5-6

Surrounded and sinking
a rope appears
will I take it or
wait for another?

January 5

44

Epiphany

"...abide in my love."
~John 15:9b

Abiding, residing in God
Looking out at the world from the place of God
Seeing with God's eyes of love.
Like the disciple resting on Jesus' breast
Close enough to feel the heart beat of God
Feel the breath that moved over the chaos
To give shape to stars and planets and all that dwells
therein.

Eve of Epiphany

Listen to me, O coastlands,
    pay attention, you people from far away!
The LORD called me before I was born,
    while I was in my mother's womb he named me.
~Isaiah 49:1

Called and named
by the Most Holy One
We walk this earth
Blessed and blessing.

He has rescued us from the power of darkness and transferred us into the kingdom of his beloved Son.
~Colossians 1:13

Suddenly we
are in a new place
while surrounded by
the old.

January 7

On the last day of the festival, the great day, while Jesus was standing there, he cried out, "Let anyone who is thirsty come to me, and let the one who believes in me drink. As the scripture has said, 'Out of the believer's heart shall flow rivers of living water.'"
~John 7:37-38

Dry, desiccated hearts
seeking
refreshing
at the living spring.

January 8

Again Jesus spoke to them, saying, "I am the light of the world. Whoever follows me will never walk in darkness but will have the light of life"
~John 8:12

I AM Bread
fresh-baked
filling your house
with scents of home
I AM Water
flowing through
the earth
satisfying your thirst
I AM Vine
breaking through
the pavement over your heart
wrapping your spirit in new growth
I AM Light
filling every corner
seeking the dawn of your soul.

January 9

then the LORD God formed man from the dust of the ground, and breathed into its nostrils the breath of life, and the man became a living being.
~Genesis 2:7

Clay doll
standing on the edge
of the river of life
Plunges into living.

Seek the LORD while he may be found,
    call upon him while he is near.
~Isaiah 55:6

The movers are
loading the furniture
from the neighbor's house
How far away
are they going?
Will we still meet for coffee?

January 11

"I have said these things to you so that my joy may be in you, and that your joy may be complete. This is my commandment, that you love one another as I have loved you. No one has greater love than this, to lay down one's life for one's friends."
~John 15:11-13

Joy completes
when I let go of my rules
for your life.

But speaking the truth in love, we must grow up in every way into him who is the head, into Christ, from whom the whole body, joined and knit together by every ligament with which it is equipped, as each part is working properly, promotes the body's growth in building up in love.
~Ephesians 4:15-16

No dropped stitches
in the knitting
of the kingdom.

Eve of 1 Epiphany

Now in Jerusalem by the Sheep Gate there is a pool, called in Hebrew Beth-zatha. One man was there who had been ill for thirty-eight years.
~John 5:2, 5

At the pool
I wait for healing waters
to shiver me well.

Week of 1 Epiphany: Sunday

From his fullness we have all received, grace upon grace.
~John 1:16

Flooding out to water the thirsty land
Bringing nutrients to the ground of being
Creation, destruction, creation.

Monday

And he cured many who were sick with various diseases, and cast out many demons; and he would not permit the demons to speak, because they knew him.
~Mark 1:34

When I
know my demons
will I
know the Holy?

Tuesday

Since, therefore, the children share flesh and blood, he himself likewise shared the same things, so that through death he might destroy the one who has the power of death, that is, the devil, and free those who all their lives were held in slavery by the fear of death.
~Hebrews 2:14-15

Chains of fear
enslave the heart
Paralyze the mind
Death will come
but fear need not.

Wednesday

Philip found Nathanael and said to him, "We have found him about whom Moses in the law and also the prophets wrote, Jesus son of Joseph from Nazareth." Nathanael said to him, "Can anything good come out of Nazareth?' Philip said to him, 'Come and see."
~John 1:45-46

Good comes knocking
at our door.
Will we open up
or stay hidden behind the locks in our minds?

Thursday

Take care, brothers and sisters, that none of you may have an evil, unbelieving heart that turns away from the living God. But exhort one another every day, as long as it is called "today," so that none of you may be hardened by the deceitfulness of sin. For we have become partners of Christ, if only we hold our first confidence firm to the end.
~Hebrews 3:12-14

God's company
is always hiring
full partners.

Friday

Indeed, the word of God is living and active, sharper than any two-edged sword, piercing until it divides soul from spirit, joints from marrow.
~Hebrews 4:12a

Word-sword
slices through
ropes and chains
cutting all that binds.

But speaking the truth in love, we must grow up in every way into him who is the head, into Christ, from whom the whole body, joined and knit together by every ligament with which it is equipped, as each part is working properly, promotes the body's growth in building itself up in love.
~Ephesians 4:1-16

Truth in love
re-tying the broken threads
in the fabric of life.

"The wind blows where it chooses, and you hear the sound of it, but you do not know where it comes from or where it goes."
~John 3:8

Gentle breezes whisper
Gusty gales blast
Wind stirs
my soul
Re-arranging the landscape.

Monday

I will remember my covenant that is between me and you and every living creature of all flesh; and the waters shall never again become a flood to destroy all flesh.
~Genesis 9:115

Floods of famine
Torrents of war
Rivers of blood
Will you remember?
Sometimes it seems God
has forgotten
or have we?

Tuesday

And we want each one of you to show the same diligence so as to realize the full assurance of hope to the very end, so that you may not become sluggish, but imitators of those who through faith and patience inherit the promises.
~Hebrews 6:11-12

Slugs slide slowly
across the garden
eating my pansies
and leaving slime.

Wednesday

A Samaritan woman came to draw water, and Jesus said to her, "Give me a drink" ... The Samaritan woman said to him, "How is it that you, a Jew, ask a drink of me, a woman of Samaria?"
~John 4:7, 9

Strange things when we thirst---
If Jewish men and Samaritan women
start talking--- where will it end!!!

Thursday

From there he moved on to the hill country on the east of Bethel, and pitched his tent, with Bethel on the west and Ai on the east; and there he built an altar to the LORD and invoked the name of the LORD.
~Genesis 12:8

Traveling through life
Building altars
and moving on.
Stones in the path mark
the presence of holiness.

Friday

Many Samaritans from that city believed in him because of the woman's testimony, "He told me everything I have ever done."
~John 4:39

Your word
becomes my word
when I know Word.

Saturday

Then Jesus ordered them to tell no one; but the more he ordered them, the more zealously they proclaimed it.
~Mark 7:36

When the ropes are pulled
the bells must ring.
The momentum
is irresistible.

"I will put my laws in their minds,
    and write them on their hearts,
and I will be their God,
    and they shall be my people."
~Hebrews 8:10b

We will not be lost
when our internal compass
is set for True North.

Monday

"It is the sabbath; it is not lawful for you to carry your mat." But he answered them, "The man who made me well, said to me, 'Take up your mat and walk.'"
~John 5:10b-11

Healing brings on
lawbreaking?

Your statutes have been like songs to me
wherever I have lived as a stranger.
~Psalm 119:54

Lullabies of comfort
in the foreign lands.
Songs of love
for lonely times.
Be still now and listen.

Wednesday

I will take no bull-calf from your stalls,
    nor he-goats out of your pens;
For all the beasts of the forest are mine,
    the herds in their thousands upon the hills.
I know every bird in the sky,
    and the creatures of the fields are in my sight.
If I were hungry, I would not tell you,
    for the whole world is mine and all that is in it.
Do you think I eat the flesh of bulls,
    or drink the blood of goats?
Offer to God a sacrifice of thanksgiving
    and make good your vows to the Most High.
~Psalm 50:9-14

Rituals will not satisfy
while there is one hungry child.

Thursday

One of his disciples, Andrew, Simon Peter's brother, said to him, "There is a boy here who has five barley loaves and two fish. But what are they among so many people?"
~John 6:8-9

A cup of water
in a desert of thirst
can open hidden wells.

Friday

It is a fearful thing to fall into the hands of the living God.
~Hebrews 10:31

Awakening to know
we are held in holiness,
Fear shakes us to our very souls.

Saturday

Then Abraham came near and said, "Will you indeed sweep away the righteous with the wicked?... Suppose ten are found there." God answered, "For the sake of ten I will not destroy it."
~Genesis 18:23, 32b

The earth continues
so ten remain.
Have you seen them?

But Lot's wife, behind him, looked back, and she
became a pillar of salt.
~Genesis 19:26

Walking away
Heavy hearted
From home---
where friends chatted
in the market,
babies were born,
Oh my beloved city
Endless tears turn me to stone.

Monday

So Abraham rose early in the morning, and took bread and a skin of water, and gave it to Hagar, putting it on her shoulder, along with the child, and sent her away. And she departed, and wandered about in the wilderness of Beer-sheba.

When the water in the skin was gone, she cast the child under one of the bushes. Then she went and sat down opposite him a good way off, about the distance of a bowshot; for she said, "Do not let me look on the death of the child." And as she sat opposite him, she lifted up her voice and wept. And God heard the voice of the boy; and the angel of God called to Hagar from heaven, and said to her, "What troubles you, Hagar? Do not be afraid; for God has heard the voice of the boy where he is. Come, lift up the boy and hold him fast with your hand, for I will make a great nation of him." Then God opened her eyes and she saw a well of water.
~Genesis 21:14-19

Ishmael and Isaac
Wilderness
Sacrifice
Death or life
Depends on where you look.

Tuesday

...for he persevered as though he saw the one who is invisible.
~Hebrews 11:27b

Faced with drowning in slavery---
Moses strides into the sea
following a promise and a memory of burning bush.

Wednesday

Therefore, since we are surrounded by so great a cloud of witnesses, let us also lay aside every weight and the sin that clings so closely, and let us run with perseverance the race that is set before us.
~Hebrews 12:1

Freed of her burdens
the horse speeds across the prairie
Leaping and bucking
in the morning sun.

Thursday

"I am not going to this festival, for my time has not yet fully come."
~John 7:8b

How to know
the moment
for speaking
or acting
Is it now?

Friday

Therefore lift your drooping hands and strengthen your weak knees, and make straight paths for your feet, so that what is lame may not be put out of joint, but rather be healed.
~Hebrews 12:12-13

Is it the path
that causes lameness
The road
that weakens the knees?

Saturday

"Truly I tell you, whoever does not receive the kingdom of God as a little child will never enter it."
~Mark 10:15

Jumping and leaping
Stumbling and falling
Giggling and laughing
Crying and weeping
With dirty hands
and untied shoes
Handful of dandelions
and gap-toothed smile
We are all welcome
Just as we are.

Week of 5 Epiphany: Sunday

Do not neglect to show hospitality to strangers, for by doing that some have entertained angels without knowing it.
~Hebrews 13:1-16

Sharing a table at Starbucks
Strangers chatting
on our separate ways
Later the barista sweeps
up the feathers along with the
crumpled napkins.

Monday

Jesus bent down and wrote with his finger on the ground.
When they kept on questioning him, he straightened up
and said to them, "Let anyone among you is without sin
be the first to throw a stone at her." And once again he
bent down and wrote on the ground.
~John 8:6b-8

Tablets on stone
written with law.
Tablets on the earth
written with mercy.

Tuesday

Do not be conformed to this world, but be transformed by the renewing of your minds.
~Romans 12:2

"She's only a bird in a gilded cage..."
Even with an open door
will I have the courage
to fly beyond
the bars of my cage?

Wednesday

Beloved, never avenge yourselves, but leave room for the wrath of God; for it is written, "Vengeance is mine, I will repay, says the LORD." No, "if your enemies are hungry, feed them; if they are thirsty, give them something to drink; for by doing this you will heap burning coals on their heads." Do not be overcome by evil, but overcome evil with good.
~Romans 12:19-21

The high tide of revenge
threatens to sink my boat.
Will the seawalker
calm the storms of fury?
I cannot row alone.

"Surely the LORD is in this place— and I did not know it!"
~Genesis 28:16b

When the Sun burns away the fog
There are no limits to our vision.

Friday

Let us therefore no longer pass judgment on one another, but resolve instead never to put a stumbling block or hindrance in the way of another.
~Romans 14:13

Words fall
from the tongue.
Stones
building walls
of division.

Saturday

Train yourself in godliness, for, while physical training is of some value, godliness is valuable in every way, holding promise for both the present life and the life to come.
~Timothy 4:7b-8

What equipment
will I find at the Spirit gym?

We are writing these things so that our joy may be complete.
~1 John 1:4

When two or three are gathered---
Joy lives in the midst
completeness in connection.

"You were born entirely in sins, and are you trying to teach us?" And they drove him out.
~John 9:34

The blind one
reads the Good News
While clergy see a beggar.

Tuesday

"I have other sheep that do not belong to this fold. I must bring them also, and they will listen to my voice."
~John 10:16

Voice of love
sings in the mind.
Calling
us all to join the song.

Wednesday

"My sheep hear my voice, I know them, and they follow me."
~John 10:27

Song floating on the air
Heard in the spaces of the noise of life
Calls the singers to join in harmony.

Thursday

Joseph to Esau, "Why should my lord be so kind to me?"
~Genesis 33:15b

Older brother betrayed by younger
Why be kind?
Why not return evil for evil?
Breaking bread requires two hands
While a stone can be thrown by one.

Friday

So the sisters sent a message to Jesus, "LORD, he whom you love is ill."
~John 11:3

Lying in graves of hatred.
Living in death,
Hearts shrivel
and harden
as we turn to stone.
Will our sisters send a message to the giver of Life?

Saturday

James and John, the sons of Zebedee, came forward to Jesus and said to him, "Teacher, we want you to do for us whatever we ask of you." And he said to them, "What is it you want me to do for you?" And they said to him, "Grant us to sit, one at your right hand and one at your left, in your glory."... When the ten heard this, they began to be angry with James and John.
~Mark 10:35-38,41

Anger flares
in jealous
rage
When privilege rules.

Happy are those who find Wisdom,
   and those who get understanding,
for her income is better than silver,
   and revenue better than gold.

She is a tree of life to those who lay hold of her;
   those who hold her fast are called happy.
The LORD by Wisdom founded the earth;
   by understanding established the heavens;
by knowledge the deeps broke open,
   and the clouds drop down the dew.
~Proverbs 3:13, 18-20

Creative face
of the holy.
Life force
of creation.
Wisdom
wonder
wellspring.

Monday

Get wisdom; get insight: do not forget, nor turn away
    from the words of my mouth.
Do not forsake her, and she will keep you;
    love her, and she will guard you.
The beginning of wisdom is this: Get wisdom,
    and what ever else you get, get insight.
Prize her highly, and she will exalt you;
    she will honor you if you embrace her.
She will place on your head a fair garland;
    she will bestow on you a beautiful crown.
~Proverbs 4:5-9

Garlands of winners.
Crowns of royalty.
Received
by all when
wisdom is an honored guest.

Tuesday

"What are we to do? This man is performing many signs. If we let him go on like this, everyone will believe in him, and the Romans will come and destroy both our holy place and our nation."
~John 11:47b-48

Safety demands sacrifice
Disturbing the peace
is a capital crime.

"The peace of God,
      it is no peace, but strife closed in the sod.
Yet let us pray for but one thing—
      the marvelous peace of God."
~Hymn #661 -- The Hymnal 1982

Wednesday

Little children, keep yourselves from idols.
~1John 5:21

Idols have a way of answering
needs of vulnerability,
Offering a shortcut,
saying "take and forget."

Does not wisdom call,
and does not understanding raise her voice?

"Take my instruction instead of silver,
and knowledge rather than choice gold;
for wisdom is better than jewels,
and all that you may desire
cannot compare with her

My fruit is better than gold, even fine gold,
and my yield than choice silver.
I walk in the way of righteousness,
along the path of justice,
endowing with wealth those who love me,
and filling their treasuries."
~Proverbs 8:1, 10-11, 19-21

Tending our soul garden
Weeding and pruning
We become the tree of life.

Friday

I am reminded of your sincere faith, a faith that lived
first in your grandmother Lois and your mother Eunice
and now, I am sure, lives in you.
~2 Timothy 1:5

Is there DNA of the soul?
Passed on to our descendents
Who will carry the genes
into the future?
Or will we need genetic engineering?

Saturday

Give instruction to the wise,
and they will become wiser still;
    teach the righteous, and they will gain in learning.
The fear of the LORD is the beginning of wisdom,
    and the knowledge of the Holy One is insight.
~Proverbs 9:9-10

Wisdom—
aware of
how much
is unknown,
opens the heart
to hear the words
of life.

The memory of the righteous is a blessing,
 but the name of the wicked will rot.
~Proverbs 10:7a

Wickedness:
Dry rot
turns timber
to dust
at a touch.

Righteousness:
Aging wood
stronger than steel beams
withstands the fire.

Monday

Better is a dinner of vegetables where love is
    than a fatted ox and hatred with it.
~Proverbs 15:17

Silk and linen
Silver and lace
Eight course dinners
Will not fill
the empty heart.

Tuesday

"So if I, your LORD and Teacher, have washed your feet, you also ought to wash one another's feet."
~John 13:14

Kneeling before me
With basin and towel
The Holy One waits.

Wednesday

As for me, I am already being poured out as a libation.
~Timothy 4:6a

Crossing the borders of life
Birth and death
Offering of water and blood
sanctifies the earth.

Thursday

Greet Prisca and Aquila, and the household of Onesiphorus. Erastus remained in Corinth; Trophimus I left ill in Miletus. .... Eubulus send greetings to you, as do Pudens and Linus and Claudia and all the brothers and sisters. The LORD be with your spirit. Grace be with you.
~2 Timothy 4:19-20, 21b-22

"I give you a new commandment, that you love one another. ... By this everyone will know that you are my disciples, if you have love for one another."
~John 13:34a, 35

Greek and Roman
Male and Female
Jewish and Gentile
Slave and Free
All are gathered at
the table
eating the Bread of Heaven
drinking the Water of Life.

Friday

Like a bad tooth or a lame foot
is trust in a faithless person in time of trouble.
~Proverbs 25:19

Betrayal
erodes the edges
of the heart
Fraying the fabric
of friendship.

Saturday

"What does it profit them if they gain the whole world, but lose or forfeit themselves?"
~Luke 9:25

Accolades
Possessions
Honors
Will not fill the empty heart.

Simon Peter and another disciple followed Jesus. Since that disciple was known to the high priest, he went with Jesus into the courtyard of the high priest, but Peter was standing outside at the gate. So the other disciple, who was known to the high priest, went out, spoke to the woman who guarded the gate, and brought Peter in. The woman said to Peter, "You are not also one of this man's disciples, are you?" He said, "I am not."
~John 18:15-17

She asks
and he answers
and now
is he in
or is he out?

Monday

"For this I was born, and for this I came into the world, to testify to the truth. Everyone who belongs to the truth listens to my voice." Pilate asked him, "What is truth?"
~John 18:37b-38

Bread and fishes
shared on a summer meadow.
Cups of water
ladled out for thirsty throats.
Banquets where all are guests.
A world without strangers.
Bent over women unfolding
The dead emerging from their caves
unbound by loving hands.
This is Truth.

Tuesday

Lent

Ah, you that turn justice to wormwood,
 and bring righteousness to the ground!
The one who made the Pleiades and Orion,
 and turns the deep darkness into the morning,
 and darkens the day into night,
who calls for the waters of the sea,
 and pours them out on the surface of the earth,
the LORD is his name,
who makes destruction flash our against the strong,
 so that destruction comes upon the fortress.
They hate the one who reproves in the gate,
 and they abhor the one who speaks the truth.
~Amos 5:7-10

Tsunamis of grace
Batter against
Barricaded hearts,
While pollution
clouds our vision.

Ash Wednesday

Be still before the Lord
    and wait patiently for him.
Do not fret yourself over the one who prospers,
    the one who succeeds in evil schemes.
Refrain from anger, leave rage alone;
    do not fret yourself; it leads only to evil.
~Psalm 37:7-9

Barbed wire of rage
Fences out love.

Thursday

Finally, beloved, whatever is true, whatever is honorable, whatever is just, whatever is pure, whatever is pleasing, whatever is commendable, if there is anything worthy of praise, think about these things.
~Philippians 4:8

+
++
+++
honor
purity
pleasure
commendable
praiseworthy---
Incense of blessing
rises to fill the earth.

Friday

Not that I am referring to being in need; for I have learned to be content with whatever I have. I know what it is to have little, and I know what it is to have plenty. In any and all circumstances I have learned the secret of being well-fed and of going hungry, of having plenty and of being in need. I can do all things through him who strengthens me.
~Philippians 4:11-13

Plenty or want
Much or little
Contentment cannot be bought.

"I do not judge anyone who hears my words and does not keep them, for I came not to judge the world, but to save the world."
~John 12:47

The Lifeguard
swims with strong strokes
to the drowning,
with no thought
of how they got into the deep water.

Week of 1 Lent: Sunday

And a voice came from heaven, "You are my Son, the Beloved; with you I am well pleased." And the Spirit immediately drove him out into the wilderness. He was in the wilderness forty days, tempted by Satan; and he was with the wild beasts; and the angels waited on him.
~Mark 1:11-13

The Beloved joins
the exile
from the Garden.

"Here comes this dreamer. Come now, let us kill him and throw him into one of the pits; then we shall say that a wild animal has devoured him, and we shall see what will become of his dreams."
~Genesis 37:19b-20

Pits await
those who speak the dream
and yet the dream will not be silenced.

Tuesday

In the morning, while it was still very dark, he got up
and went out to a deserted place, and there he prayed.
~Mark 1:35

What is it about deserted places
that calls us to prayer?
Stripped
Alone
In the dark
The heart beats
the rhythm of my song.

Wednesday

Then some people came, bringing to him a paralyzed
man, carried by four of them.
~Mark 2:3

Four strong friends
to carry me
When I cannot rise.

Thursday

"No one sews a piece of unshrunk cloth on an old cloak; otherwise, the patch pulls away from it, the new from the old, and a worse tear is made. And no one puts new wine into old wineskins; otherwise, the wine will burst the skins, and the wine is lost, and so are the skins; but one puts new wine into fresh wineskins."
~Mark 2:13-22

Moments come
when old and new
cannot meet.

Friday

Where can I go then from your spirit?
   where can I flee from your presence?
If I climb up to heaven, you are there;
   if I make the grave my bed, you are there also.
If I take the wings of the morning
   and dwell in the uttermost parts of the sea,
Even there your hand will lead me
   and your right hand will hold me fast.
~Psalm 139:6-9

child lost in chaos
reaches out in terror
to find safety in her mother's hand

Saturday

And Pharaoh said to Joseph, "See, I have set you over all the land of Egypt." Removing his signet ring from his hand, Pharaoh put it on Joseph's hand; he arrayed him in garments of fine linen, and put a gold chain around his neck. He had him ride in the chariot of his second-in-command; and they cried out in front of him, "Bow the knee!"
~Genesis 41:41-43a

Revolutions of life
Turn the one on his knees
to the one to whom all bow
Strange turnings
from day to day
Will we remember those days of aching knees?

Whenever the unclean spirits saw him, they fell down
before him and shouted, "You are the Son of God!"
~Mark 3:11

Fragmentation
recognizes wholeness.
Disintegration
cries out to
the weaver of souls.

Monday

Again he entered the synagogue, and a man was there who had a withered hand. They watched him to see whether he would cure him on the sabbath, so that they might accuse him. And he said to the man who had the withered hand, "Come forward." Then he said to them, "Is it lawful to do good or to do harm on the sabbath, to save life or to kill?" But they were silent. He looked around at them with anger; he was grieved at their hardness of heart and said to the man, "Stretch out your hand." He stretched it out, and his hand was restored.
~Mark 3:1-5

Anger and grief
fuel the fire
of restoration.

Tuesday

"A sower went out to sow. And as he sowed, some seed fell on the path.... Other seed fell on rocky ground.... Other seed fell among thorns.... Other seed fell into good soil..."
~Mark 4:3-4a, 5, 7, 8

Can seeds grow legs
and scramble to a better place?

Wednesday

"All things are lawful for me," but not all things are beneficial. "All things are lawful for me," I will not be dominated by anything.... Or do you not know that your body is a temple of the Holy Spirit within you?
~1 Corinthians 6:12, 19

The law says yes
but justice says no.
Rules do not rule
in the temple of the spirit.

A great windstorm arose, and the waves beat into the boat, so that the boat was already being swamped. But he was in the stern, asleep on the cushion; and they woke him up and said to him, "Teacher, do you not care that we are perishing?" He woke up and rebuked the wind, and said to the sea, "Peace! Be still!" Then the wind ceased, and there was a dead calm. He said to them, "Why are you afraid? Have you still no faith?" And they were filled with great awe and said to one another, "Who then is this, that even the wind and the sea obey him?"
~Mark 4:37-41

Eye of the hurricane
Spreads peace and calm
into the storms of my life.

Friday

They came to Jesus and saw the demoniac sitting there, clothed and in his right mind, the very man who had had the legion; and they were afraid.
~Mark 5:15

We fear the one
who comes back
from the edges of the void.
We cannot bear the knowing.

Saturday

[Joseph] commanded the steward of his house, "Fill the men's sacks with food, as much as they can carry, and put each man's money in the top of his sack. Put my cup, the silver cup, in the top of the sack of the youngest, with his money for the grain."
~Genesis 44:1-2

The victim becomes the perpetrator
in the game of retribution.
How long will Joseph live
from the pit?
How long will he be enslaved
to his anger?

Week of 3 Lent: Sunday

And a large crowd followed him and pressed in on him. Now there was a woman who had been suffering from hemorrhages for twelve years. ... She had heard about Jesus, and came up behind him in the crowd and touched his cloak.
~Mark 5:24—25, 27

Isolated and alone
Woman of blood
pours herself towards
the fabric of life.

Dewdrop of hope
slips down the thread
to the woman
with outstretched hands.

Monday

They said, "Where did this man get all this? What is this wisdom that has been given to him? What deeds of power are being done by his hands! Is not this the carpenter, the son of Mary and brother of James and Joses and Judas and Simon, and are not his sisters here with us?" And they took offense at him.
~Mark 6:2b-3

Though you have wisdom
and can heal us
We have to see
your PhD.

Tuesday

Knowledge puffs up, but love builds up.
~1 Corinthians 8:1b

Filling the fragile
skin of the balloon
with great breaths of knowledge
Blowing and blowing
It POPS!!!
Bits of what might have been
rain down on the party.

Wednesday

The apostles gathered around Jesus, and told him all that they had done and taught. He said to them, "Come away to a deserted place all by your selves and rest a while." For many were coming and going, and they had no leisure even to eat.
~Mark 6:30-46

The invitation
goes out
to all
the frantic lives
"Come away
and rest."

Thursday

Do you not know that in a race the runners all compete, but only one receives the prize? Run in such a way that you may win it. Athletes exercise self-control in all things; they do it to receive a perishable wreath, but we an imperishable one.
~1 Corinthians 9:24-25

In this race
all receive
the prize
before they even begin.

Friday

LORD, you have been our refuge
    from one generation to another.
Before the mountains were brought forth,
or the land and the earth were born,
    from age to age you are God.
You turn us back to the dust and say,
    "Go back, O child of earth."
For a thousand years in your sight are like yesterday
        when it is past
    and like a watch in the night.
~Psalm 90:1-4

The years which seemed so long
in their days
have passed into time
speeding away.
Fragments of memories
float up like pieces
of old ships
broken on the rocks of life.
Still they carry their golden cargo.

Saturday

We know that the whole creation has been groaning in labor pains until now; and not only the creation, but we ourselves, who have the first fruits of the Spirit, groan inwardly while we wait for adoption, the redemption of our bodies.

~Romans 8:22-23

The infant
suffers the labor pains
of her own birth.

Simeon and Levi are brothers;
 weapons of violence are their swords.
May I never come into their council;
 may I not be joined to their company—
for in their anger they killed men,
 and at their whim they hamstrung oxen.
Cursed be their anger, for it is fierce,
 and their wrath, for it is cruel!
I will divide them in Jacob,
 and scatter them in Israel.
~Genesis 49:5-7

The company we keep
The counsel we take
Curse or blessing?

Monday

Then he charged them, saying to them, "I am about to be gathered to my people. Bury me with my ancestors— in the cave in the field of Ephron the Hittite, in the cave in the field at Machpelah, near Mamre, in the land of Canaan, in the field that Abraham bought from Ephron the Hittite as a burial site. There Abraham and his wife Sarah were buried; there Isaac and his wife Rebekah were buried; and there I buried Leah— the field and the cave that is in it were purchased from the Hittites." When Jacob ended his charge to his sons, he drew up his feet into the bed, breathed his last, and was gathered to his people.
~Genesis 49:29-33

Home of the heart
in the ground of my people.
Where is the true home?

He took the blind man by the hand and led him out of the village; and when he had put saliva on his eyes and laid his hands on him, he asked him, "Can you see anything?" And the man looked up and said, "I can see people, but they look like trees, walking." Then Jesus laid his hands on his eyes again; and he looked intently and his sight was restored, and he saw everything clearly.
~Mark 8:23-25

Eyes opened by love
see brothers and sisters
where once only objects bustled by.

Wednesday

The king of Egypt said to the Hebrew midwives, one of whom was named Shiphrah and the other Puah, "When you act as midwives to the Hebrew women, and see them on the birthstool, if it is a boy, kill him; but if it is a girl, she shall live." But the midwives feared God; they did not do as the king of Egypt commanded them, but they let the boys live. So the king of Egypt summoned the midwives and said to them, "Why have you done this, and allowed the boys to live?" The midwives said to Pharaoh, "Because the Hebrew women are not like the Egyptian women; for they are vigorous and give birth before the midwife comes to them." So God dealt well with the midwives; and the people multiplied and became very strong. And because the midwives feared God, he gave them families.
~Exodus 1:15-21

Drop by drop
the water wears away the rock
The powerless collude
to overcome power.

Thursday

If I speak in the tongues of mortals and of angels, but do not have love, I am a noisy gong or a clanging cymbal. And if I have prophetic powers, and understand all mysteries and all knowledge, and if I have all faith, so as to remove mountains, but do not have love, I am nothing. If I give away all my possessions, and if I hand over my body so that I may boast, but do not have love, I gain nothing.
~1 Corinthians 13:1-3

Nothing plus nothing
equals nothing
Love is the sum of all.

Friday

Immediately the father of the child cried out, "I believe; help my unbelief!"
~Mark 9:24

My hand tires
and cramps
around the crayon
as I struggle
to complete the picture.
Vast unfilled spaces spread out before me.

Saturday

Do not be conformed to this world, but be transformed by the renewing of your minds, so that you may discern what is the will of God— what is good and acceptable and perfect.

~Romans 12:2

Pushed and pulled
by the pressures of the world.
The fire of the holy
hardens the clay
to its intended shape.

Week of 5 Lent: Sunday

There are doubtless many different kinds of sounds in the world, and nothing is without sound. If then I do not know the meaning of a sound, I will be a foreigner to the speaker and the speaker a foreigner to me. So with yourselves; since you are eager for spiritual gifts, strive to excel in them for building up the church.
~1 Corinthians 14:10-12

How are we to understand
when we do not know the language?
Especially the language of hope?

Monday

But the king of Egypt said to them, "Moses and Aaron, why are you taking the people away from their work? Get to your labors!" Pharaoh continued, "Now they are more numerous than the people of the land and yet you want them to stop working!" That same day Pharaoh commanded the taskmaster of the people, as well as their supervisors, "You shall no longer give the people straw to make bricks, as before; let them go and gather straw for themselves. But you shall require of them the same quantity of bricks as they have made previously; do not diminish it, for they are lazy; that is why they cry, 'Let us go and offer sacrifice to our God.' Let heavier work be laid on them; then they will labor at it and pay no attention to deceptive words."
~Exodus 5:4-9

Words of liberation
become words of deception
in the ears of the powerful.

Tuesday

Truly I tell you, whoever does not receive the kingdom of God as a little child will never enter it.
~Mark 10:15

Children:
Fearful and brave
Greedy and loving
Crying and laughing
Seeing wonders all around.

I look to my right hand
and find no one who knows me;
    I have no place to flee to,
    and no one cares for me.
I cry out to you, O LORD;
    I say, "You are my refuge,
    my portion in the land of the living."
~Psalm 142:4-5

Desolate stranger
seeking solace
Surrounded by life
Alone
As a child lost in a crowd.

Thursday

"You know that among the Gentiles those whom they recognize as their rulers lord it over them, and their great ones are tyrants over them. But it is not so among you; but whoever wishes to become great among you must be your servant, and whoever wishes to be first among you must be slave of all."
~Mark 10:42b-44

Ruling or serving
Who is recognized as "great"?
Whose name will I find in history books?

Even though our outer nature is wasting away, our inner nature is being renewed day by day.
~2 Corinthians 4:16b

Frailty and infirmity
Awaken the knowledge
of our common destination.

Saturday

As [Jesus] came near and saw the city, he wept over it, saying, "If you, even you, had only recognized on this day the things that make for peace!"
~Luke 19:41-42a

If Only –
the cry comes
when all is lost.

Blessed be the God and Father of our LORD Jesus Christ, the Father of mercies and the God of all consolation, who consoles us in all our affliction, so that we may be able to console those who are in any affliction with the consolations with which we ourselves are consoled by God.
~2 Corinthians 1:3-4

We sit
in silence
known and knowing.
Companions in pain.

Monday

It is God who establishes us with you in Christ and has anointed us by putting his seal on us and giving us his Spirit in our hearts as a first installment.
~2 Corinthians 1:21-22

Householder God
Makes a down payment on us
Trusting us to become a home.

"When the season came, he sent a slave to the tenants to collect from them his share of the produce of the vineyard. But they seized him, and beat him, and sent him away empty-handed."
~Mark 12:2-3

How long will we beat and kill
those who come for a share
of abundance?

Wednesday

Because there is one bread, we who are many are one body, for we all partake of the one bread.
~1 Corinthians 10:17

Seeds grow wheat
Grain ground to flour
Mixed and baked
Into One
Broken and shared
The spiral dance
Gathering and breaking
Gathering and breaking.

Maundy Thursday

The steadfast love of the LORD never ceases,
his mercies never come to an end;
they are new every morning;
great is your faithfulness."
~Lamentations 3:22-23

In the darkness of my days
Your hands on mine
Your sweet words
Bring morning
into my soul.

Good Friday

160

Those who were my enemies without cause
    have hunted me like a bird;
they flung me alive into a pit
    and hurled stones on me;
water closed over my head;
    I said, "I am lost."
I called on your name, O LORD,
    from the depths of the pit;
you heard my plea. "Do not close your ear
    to my cry for help, but give me relief!"
You came near when I called on you;
    you said, "Do not fear!'"
You have taken up my cause, O LORD,
    you have redeemed my life.
~Lamentations 3:52-58

Fear drowns
hearts and minds
Building walls
against the sun.

Easter

But they urged him strongly, saying, "Stay with us, because it is almost evening and the day is now nearly over." So he went in to stay with them. When he was at the table with them, he took bread, blessed and broke it, and gave it to them. Then their eyes were opened, and they recognized him; and he vanished from their sight.
~Luke 24:29-31

At table
With bread
Love offered
and received.
Alleluia!

Easter Week: Sunday

Then Moses called all the elders of Israel and said to them, "Go, select lambs for your families, and slaughter the passover lamb. Take a bunch of hyssop, dip it in the blood that is in the basin, and touch the lintel and the two doorposts with the blood in the basin. None of you shall go outside the door of your house until morning. For the LORD will pass through to strike down the Egyptians; when he sees the blood on the lintel and on the two doorposts, the LORD will pass over that door and will not allow the destroyer to enter your houses to strike you down."

~Exodus 12:21-23

Blood of the lambs
on the doorposts
Birthing a people
to life or death?

If there is no resurrection of the dead, then Christ has not been raised; and if Christ has not been raised, then our proclamation has been in vain and your faith has been in vain.
~1 Corinthians 15:13-14

Is faith
the cake
that has fallen
because the oven door
was slammed in the baking?
Is faith
the bread
unable to rise
without the yeast?

Tuesday

And suddenly there was a great earthquake; for an angel of the LORD, descending from heaven, came and rolled back the stone and sat on it. His appearance was like lightning, and his clothing white as snow. For fear of him the guards shook and became like dead men. But the angel said to the women, "Do not be afraid."
~Matthew 28:2-5

Rolling earth
shakes loose
the stones
over tombs trying
to contain love.

"And remember, I am with you always, to the end of the age."
~Matthew 28:20

remember, I AM
I AM with you
to the end, I AM.

Thursday

Now it was Mary Magdalene, Joanna, Mary the mother of James, and the other women with them who told this to the apostles. But these words seemed to them an idle tale, and they did not believe them. But Peter got up and ran to the tomb.
~Luke 24:10-12

Flinging their words
against a wall of unbelief
Only Peter
hears and hopes.

Friday

"But understand this: if the owner of the house had known in what part of the night the thief was coming, he would have stayed awake and would not have let his house be broken into. Therefore you also must be ready, for the Son of Man is coming at an unexpected hour."
~Matthew 24:43-44

The thief of hearts
is waiting for that unguarded
moment
in barricaded souls
and locked doors.

Saturday

Then Moses stretched out his hand over the sea. The
LORD drove the sea back by a strong east wind all night
and turned the sea into dry land; and the waters were
divided. The Israelites went into the sea on dry ground,
the waters forming a wall for them on their right and
on their left.
~Exodus 14:21-22

From blood on the lintels
and doorposts
through the waters
parted by the midwife God
the infant nation
is birthed onto the far shore
of their new life.

Week 2 of Easter: Sunday

"And I will ask the Father, and he will give you another Advocate, to be with you forever. This is the Spirit of truth, whom the world cannot receive, because it neither sees the Spirit of truth nor knows the Spirit of truth. You know the spirit, because it abides with you, and it will be in you."
~John 14:16-17

Our Pilate-self asks,
"What is truth?"
Truth cannot live in hearts of stone
Power hangs truth on the cross.

Monday

Then the prophet Miriam, Aaron's sister, took a tambourine in her hand; and all the women went out after her with tambourines and with dancing. And Miriam sang to them:

"Sing to the LORD, for he has
triumphed gloriously;
horse and rider he has thrown into the sea."
~Exodus 15:20-21

Freedom unbinds the feet
sings and dances
its way into the world.

Tuesday

Once you were not a people,
   but now you are God's people;
once you had not received mercy,
   but now you have received mercy.
~1 Peter 2:10

Sweeping up
the scraps of lives
Forming God-nation
with hearts of mercy.

Wednesday

Slaves, accept the authority of your masters with all deference, not only those who are kind and gentle but also those who are harsh. For it is a credit to you if, being aware of God, you endure pain while suffering unjustly. If you endure when you are beaten for doing wrong, what credit is that? But if you endure when you do right and suffer for it, you have God's' approval.
~1 Peter 2:18-21

Can you hear the cock crow?
Once again
Peter
gets it wrong.

"Nevertheless I tell you the truth: it is to your advantage that I go away, the Advocate will not come to you; but if I go, I will send him to you.

When the Spirit of truth comes, he will guide into all the truth; for he will not speak on his own, but will speak whatever he hears, and will declare to you the things that are to come."
~John 16:7, 13

Where will I hear
this voice of truth?
How can I be sure
in the noise of life?

Friday

"Ask and you will receive, so that your joy may be complete."
~John 16:24b

Joy
for the asking
Amazing
Rain for dry fields
Wildflowers rioting in spring
What will you ask?

Saturday

Now after [Jesus] rose early on the first day of the week, he appeared first to Mary Magdalene, from whom he had cast out seven demons.
~Mark 16:9

Seven demons
what were they?
Hunger?
Anger?
Loneliness?
Fear?
Unworthiness?
Emptiness?
Despair?

A perfect number
of demons
filled Magdalene
until the Perfect One
entered her life.

Week of 3 Easter: Sunday

LORD, who may dwell in your tabernacle?
    who may abide upon your holy hill?
~Psalm 15:1

What keys
do we need
to open the door
to home?

For my life is wasted with grief,
and my years with sighing;
~Psalm 31:10a

When will the sun
break through the clouds
and thickly clinging fog?
Step by step
Trust the path.

Tuesday

"His winnowing fork is in his hand, and he will clear his threshing floor and will gather his wheat into the granary; but the chaff he will burn with unquenchable fire."
~Matthew 3:12

Gathering us
into the heart of the holy
Our chaff
burns away
in the fires of love.

Be still before the LORD
    and wait patiently for God.
Do not fret yourself over the one who prospers,
    the one who succeeds in evil schemes.
Refrain from anger, leave rage alone;
    do not fret yourself; it leads only to evil.
~Psalm 37:7-9

Turning
away from
rage.
I walk the beach---
The Pacific in storm
stills the hurricanes of my heart.

Thursday

Therefore do not let anyone condemn you in matters of food and drink or of observing festivals, new moons, or sabbaths. These are only a shadow of what is to come, but the substance belongs to Christ. Do not let anyone disqualify you, insisting on self-abasement and worship of angels, dwelling on visions, puffed up without cause by a human way of thinking, and not holding fast to the head, from whom the whole body, nourished and held together by its ligaments and sinews, grows with a growth that is from God.

If with Christ you died to the elemental spirits of the universe, why do you live as if you still belonged to the world? Why do you submit to regulations, "Do not handle, Do not taste, Do not touch"? All these regulations refer to things that perish with use; they are simply human commands and teachings. These have indeed an appearance of wisdom in promoting self-imposed piety, humility, and severe treatment of the body, but they are of no value in checking self-indulgence.
~Colossians 2:16-23

Snowmen
melt in the
heat of the Son.

As he walked by the Sea of Galilee, he saw two brothers, Simon, who is called Peter, and Andrew his brother, casting a net into the sea—for they were fishermen. And he said to them, "Follow me, and I will make you fish for people." Immediately they left their nets and followed him. As he went from there, he saw two other brothers, James son of Zebedee and his brother John, in the boat with their father Zebedee, mending their nets, and he called them. Immediately they left the boat and their father, and followed him.

Jesus went throughout Galilee, teaching in their synagogues and proclaiming the good news of the kingdom and curing every disease and every sickness among the people. So his fame spread throughout all Syria, and they brought to him all the sick, those who were afflicted with various diseases and pains, demoniacs, epileptics, and paralytics, and he cured them. And great crowds followed him from Galilee, the Decapolis, Jerusalem, Judea, and from beyond the Jordan.

~Matthew 4:18-25

Nets of healing
haul in the catch
with ropes of good news.

Saturday

The apostles gathered around Jesus, and told him all that they had done and taught. He said to them, "Come away to a deserted place all by yourselves and rest a while." For many were coming and going, and they had no leisure even to eat. And they went away in the boat to a deserted place by themselves.
~Mark 6:30-32

In silent places
tangles of the soul
can be released.

He took the calf that they had made, burned it with fire, ground it to powder, scattered it on the water, and made the Israelites drink it.
~Exodus 32:20

The idols of our time
make a bitter brew.

Monday

Bless the LORD, O my soul,
  and all that is within me, bless his holy Name.
~Psalm 103:1

Sinews and muscles
Heart and lungs
Blood vessels and lymph system
Bones and cartilage
Singing a song of blessing
Bursting out with Alleluia!!!

Tuesday

Thus the LORD used to speak to Moses face to face, as
one speaks to a friend.
~Exodus 33:11

Friends
chatting
and gossiping
catching up on the news
cup of tea
maybe a cookie?
The Almighty One
who comes in cloud and lightning
fire and wind.
Creator of the stars.
Friends?

Wednesday

"You have heard that it was said to those of ancient times, 'You shall not murder'; and 'whoever murders shall be liable to judgment.' But I say to you that if you are angry with a brother or sister, you will be liable to judgment; and if you insult a brother or sister, you will be liable to the council; and if you say, 'You fool,' you will be liable to the hell of fire."
~Matthew 5:21-22

Bows of anger
Arrows of insults
Split the heart

Thursday

"Let your word be 'Yes, Yes' or 'No, No'; anything more than this comes from the evil one."
~Matthew 5:37

Stuck in the muddy rut
The spinning tire
digs deeper
and deeper
Leaving me buried up to the door panels
Unable to get out and walk.

Friday

"But I say to you, Love your enemies and pray for those who persecute you, so that you may be children of your Father in heaven; for he makes his sun rise on the evil and on the good, and sends rain on the righteous and on the unrighteous."
~Matthew 5:44-45

Sun and rain
gifts for growth
weeds, wheat, and wildflowers
all loved.

Saturday

When they heard this, all in the synagogue were filled with rage. They got up, drove him out of town, and led him to the brow of the hill on which their town was built, so that they might hurl him off the cliff. But he passed through the midst of them and went on his way.
~Luke 4:28-30

Enraged by truth
we seek to fling it over
the edge of our minds
and out of our hearts
But truth continues --- walking on its way.

Week of 5 Easter: Sunday

You have noted my lamentation;
put my tears into your bottle;
    are they not recorded in your book?
~Psalm 56:8

Even our tears
are treasured.

Monday

"And do not bring us to the time of trial,
but rescue us from the evil one."
~Matthew 6:13

Please God,
no pop quizzes this week.
I am barely passing
this life class.
The lessons seem to come
so quickly.

Tuesday

You shall not defraud your neighbor; you shall not steal; and you shall not keep for yourself the wages of a laborer until morning. You shall not revile the deaf or put a stumbling block before the blind; you shall fear your God: I am the LORD. You shall not render an unjust judgment; you shall not be partial to the poor or defer to the great: with justice you shall judge your neighbor. You shall not go around as a slanderer among your people, and you shall not profit by the blood of your neighbor: I am the LORD. You shall not hate in your heart anyone of your kin; you shall not reprove your neighbor, or you will incur guilt yourself. You shall not take vengeance or bear a grudge against any of your people, but you shall love your neighbor as yourself: I am the LORD."
~Leviticus 19:13-18

I AM
not greed
not false
not thief
not hate
I AM
abundance
justice
love
eternal
I AM the LORD your God
Come my beloved ones— join me— be blessed and blessing.

Wednesday

"So do not worry about tomorrow, for tomorrow will bring worries of its own. Today's trouble is enough for today."
~Matthew 6:34

Multiple projections
on the screen
overlap
to blur
the picture.

Thursday

"Do not judge, so that you may not be judged. For with the judgment you make you will be judged, and the measure you give will be the measure you get. Why do you see the speck in your neighbor's eye, but do not notice the log in your own eye?"
~Matthew 7:1-3

The log
in my eye
is so large
It is all I see
when I look at others.

"Every tree that does not bear good fruit is cut down and thrown into the fire. Thus you will know them by their fruits. Not everyone who says to me, 'LORD, LORD,' will enter the kingdom of heaven, but only the one who does the will of my Father in heaven."
~Matthew 7:19-21

It is the walk
and not the talk.

Saturday

And he said to them, "Take care! Be on your guard against all kinds of greed; for one's life does not consist in the abundance of possessions."
~Luke 12:15

Greed slips
into my life
so smoothly.
An unguarded moment
and it has consumed me.

O Lord God of hosts,
    how long will you be angered
    despite the prayers of your people?
You have fed them with the bread of tears;
    you have given them bowls of tears to drink.
You have made us the derision of our neighbors,
    and our enemies laugh us to scorn.
Restore us, O God of hosts;
    show the light of your countenance,
        and we shall be saved.
~Psalm 80:4-7

Are YOU hiding your
face so we will not see your tears?

Monday

I will break your proud glory, and I will make your sky like iron and your earth like copper.
~Leviticus 26:19

An early warning
On Global Warming?
Pride and power
exact a price
paid in earth and sky.

Tuesday

When they had crossed, Elijah said to Elisha, "Tell me what I may do for you, before I am taken from you." Elisha said, "Please let me inherit a double share of your spirit." He responded, "You have asked a hard thing; yet, if you see me as I am being taken from you, it will be granted you; if not, it will not."
~2 Kings 2:9-10

With beeps, clicks, and wavy green lines
the machines
tell me one last story
of life.
You slip out towards
your future
leaving gifts
of wonder.

Eve of Ascension

Because he himself was tested by what he suffered, he is able to help those who are being tested.
~Hebrews 2:18

"And remember, I am with you always, to the end of the age."
~Matthew 28:20b

Easier to trust
the One who
has already
been through
the storms
of life.

Ascension Day: Thursday

There is no Holy One like the Lord,
    no one besides you;
    there is no Rock like our God.
Talk no more so very proudly,
    let not arrogance come from your mouth;
for the Lord is a God of knowledge,
    and by him actions are weighed.
~1 Samuel 2:2-3

Proud words
return
to strike the heart
and bring dust to the mouth.

Friday

So then you are no longer strangers and aliens, but you are citizens with the saints and also members of the household of God, built upon the foundation of the apostles and prophets, with Christ Jesus himself as the cornerstone. In him the whole structure is joined together and grows into a holy temple in the LORD; in whom you also are built together spiritually into a dwelling place for God.
~Ephesians 2:19-22

Cornerstone
Foundation
First story
Second story
and soon we have a house for the Holy.

Saturday

Then Moses said, "I must turn aside and look at this great sight, and see why the bush is not burned up."
~Exodus 3:3

Promised land
and holy ground
happen
in moments
of distraction.
What if Moses had kept on going with the sheep?

Yours are the heavens; the earth also is yours;
     you laid the foundations of the world
          and all that is in it.
You have made the north and the south;
     Tabor and Hermon rejoice in your Name.
You have a mighty arm;
     strong is your hand and high is your right hand.
Righteousness and justice are the foundations
          of your throne;
     love and truth go before your face.
Happy are the people who know the festal shout!
     they walk, O Lord, in the light of your presence.
They rejoice daily in your Name;
     they are jubilant in your righteousness.
For you are the glory of their strength,
     and by your favor our might is exalted.
Truly, the Lord is our ruler;
     The Holy One of Israel is our King.
~Psalm 89:11-18

The chair sits
solidly
on legs of justice.

Monday

Samuel said, "How can I go? If Saul hears of it, he will kill me." And the LORD said, "Take a heifer with you, and say, 'I have come to sacrifice to the LORD.'"
~1 Samuel 16:2

God of trickiness?
Sneaking Samuel
through Saul's defenses
Intent on anointing David.
Not just the heifer was sacrificed that day.

Tuesday

I therefore, the prisoner of the LORD, beg you to lead a life worthy of the calling to which you have been called, with all humility and gentleness, with patience, bearing with one another in love, making every effort to maintain the unity of the Spirit in the bond of peace.
~Ephesians 4:1-3

Labor of love
births bonds
of peace.

Let no evil talk come out of your mouths, but only what is useful for building up, as there is need, so that your words may give grace to those who hear.
~Ephesians 4:29

Evil slips smoothly
from the tongue
going out
to search and destroy.

Thursday

I will put my law within them, and I will write it on their hearts; and I will be their God, and they shall be my people.
~Jeremiah 31:33b

Maybe the words
on the pages of my heart
need an Editor.

Friday

and the nations shall know that I am the LORD, says the Lord GOD, when through you I display my holiness before their eyes. ... A new heart I will give you, and a new spirit I will put within you; and I will remove from your body the heart of stone and give you a heart of flesh.

~Ezekiel 36:23b, 26

Stony hearts
cannot bleed.

Saturday

Pentecost

Moses brought the people out of the camp to meet God.
They took their stand at the foot of the mountain.
~Exodus 19:17

Do we have any idea
of what will happen
if we stand
at the foot of a mountain
seeking to meet God?

Eve of Pentecost

"God is spirit, and those who worship God must worship
in spirit and in truth."
~John 4:24

cathedrals and churches
tabernacles and mosques
temples and shrines—
cages cannot contain the wild God.
The Holy One dances out into the world.

Day of Pentecost: Sunday

Sing and rejoice, O daughter Zion! For lo, I will come and dwell in your midst, says the LORD.
~Zechariah 2:10

How far
shall we spread
our tent stakes
to make room
for such a guest?

Happy are those who act with justice
   and always do what is right!
Remember me, O Lord,
with the favor you have for your people,
   and visit me with your saving help;
~Psalm 106:3-4

Holiness
Visits
in every act
of justice.

They went out from us, but they did not belong to us; for if they had belonged to us, they would have remained with us. But by going out they made it plain that none of them belongs to us.
~1 John 2:19

The staying one is leaving
the leaving one is staying
who belongs, who remains.

Wednesday

These twelve Jesus sent out with the following instructions: "See, I am sending you out like sheep into the midst of wolves; so be wise as serpents and innocent as doves."
~Matthew 10:5,16

Wolves shocked by
sheep in the pack
Curling up with the pups.

"Are not two sparrows sold for a penny? Yet not one of them will fall to the ground apart from your Father. And even the hairs of your head are all counted. So be not afraid."
~Matthew 10:29-31

Lives
like frightened birds
flutter against the storms of life
But the One who counts hairs
Will bear them up and bring them to nest.

Friday

"And whoever gives even a cup of cold water to one of these little ones in the name of a disciple— truly I tell you, none of these will lose their reward."
~Matthew 10:42

In the desert places of my life
You offer the cup
Living water strengthens me
to continue my journey.

Saturday

"Where were you when I laid the
        foundation of the earth?
On what were its bases sunk,
    or who laid its cornerstone
when the morning stars sang together
    and all the heavenly beings shouted for joy?
Or who shut in the sea with doors
    when it burst out from the womb?
when I made the clouds its garment,
    and thick darkness its swaddling band,
and prescribed bounds for it,
    and set bars and doors,
and said, 'Thus far shall you come, and no farther,
    and here shall your proud waves be stopped'?"
~Job 38:4a, 6-11

Where was I?
When stars sang
and the waters ran free?
Was I there?

Trinity Sunday

Happy are those who find wisdom,
    and those who get understanding,
for her income is better than silver,
    and her revenue better than gold.
She is more precious than jewels,
    and nothing you desire can compare with her.
Long life is in her right hand;
    in her left hand are riches and honor.
Her ways are ways of pleasantness,
    and all her paths are peace.
She is a tree of life to those who lay hold of her;
    those who hold her fast are called happy.
The LORD by wisdom founded the earth;
    by understanding established the heavens;
by his knowledge the deeps broke open,
    and the clouds drop down the dew.
~Proverbs 3:13-20

Lifetime annuity
for an investment
in Wisdom.

Beloved, let us love one another, because love is from God; everyone who loves is born of God and knows God.
~1 John 4:7

Love begets love.

Tuesday

When John heard in prison what the Messiah was doing, he sent word by his disciples and said to him, "Are you the one who is to come, or are we to wait for another?"
~Matthew 11:2-3

In a prison
of doubt
waiting
for the key.

One night they both dreamed— the cupbearer and the baker of the king of Egypt, who were confined in the prison-each his own dream, and each dream with its own meaning. When Joseph came to them in the morning, he saw that they were troubled. So he asked Pharaoh's officers, who were with him in custody in his master's house, "Why are your faces downcast today?" They said to him, "We have had dreams, and there is no one to interpret them." And Joseph said to them, "Do not interpretations belong to God?"
~Genesis 40:5-8

Door of dreams
Knock
Enter
Seek

Thursday

My heart, therefore, is glad, and my spirit rejoices;
     my body also shall rest in hope.
For you will not abandon me to the grave,
     nor let your holy one see the Pit.
You will show me the path of life;
     in your presence there is fullness of joy,
     and in your right hand are pleasures for evermore.
~Psalm 16:9-11

Unfurled hand
opens to reveal
gifts and treasures
pouring like sand
through a child's fingers.

Friday

227

For the bed is too short to stretch oneself on it,
and the covering too narrow to wrap oneself in it.
~Isaiah 28:20

A restless,
shivering night
in a place that does not fit
comes to an end
with a virgin
wrapping a baby
in bands of cloth.
We will find our rest
in the manger
of God's compassion.

Saturday

Praise the LORD from the earth,
    you sea-monsters and all deeps;
Fire and hail, snow and fog,
    tempestuous wind, doing his will;
Mountains and hills,
    fruit trees and all cedars;
Wild beasts and all cattle,
    creeping things and winged birds;...
~ Psalm 148:7-10

My small car
creeps through the
fog and snow
seeking home.
Warmth of the heater
keeping out the great cold
universe of wilderness.

Proper 3: Sunday
Week of the Sunday closest to May 25

Show me your ways, O LORD,
   and teach me your paths.
Lead me in your truth and teach me,
   for you are the God of my salvation;
   in you have I trusted all the day long.
Remember, O LORD, your compassion and love,
   for they are from everlasting.
~Psalm 25:3-5

If the Holy One forgets compassion and love
what will hold the world together?

Monday

He reached down from on high and grasped me;
    he drew me out of great waters.
~Psalm 18:17

In the depths of despair
A touch calms
and gives hope.

Come now, let us argue it out, says the LORD.
~Isaiah 1:18

Don't just cower
in corners.
Stand up
Come over for
a cup of coffee
and let's argue
into the night.

Wednesday

Do not fret yourself because of evildoers;
>   do not be jealous of those who do wrong.
For they shall soon wither like the grass,
>   and like the green grass fade away.
Put your trust in the LORD and do good;
>   dwell in the land and feed on its riches.
Take delight in the LORD,
>   and he shall give you your heart's desire.
Commit your way to the LORD
>   and put your trust in him,
>   and he will bring it to pass.
He will make your righteousness as clear as the light
>   and your just dealing as the noonday.
Be still before the LORD
>   and wait patiently for him.
Do not fret yourself over the one who prospers,
>   the one who succeeds in evil schemes.
Refrain from anger, leave rage alone;
>   do not fret yourself; it leads only to evil.
~Psalm 37:1-9

Anger and rage
Unlock the door
to halls of mirrors.

Thursday

In you, O LORD, have I taken refuge;
let me never be put to shame;
    deliver me in your righteousness.
Incline your ear to me;
    make haste to deliver me.
Be my strong rock, a castle to keep me safe,
for you are my crag and my stronghold;
    for the sake of your Name, lead me and guide me.
Take me out of the net
that they have secretly set for me,
    for you are my tower of strength.
Into your hands I commend my spirit,
    for you have redeemed me,
    O LORD, O God of truth.
~Psalm 31:1-5

Storms rage
as we fly
to safety.

Friday

A crowd was sitting around him; and they said to him, "Your mother and your brothers and sisters are outside, asking for you." And he replied, "Who are my mother and my brothers?" And looking at those who sat around him, he said, "Here are my mother and my brothers! Whoever does the will of God is my brother and sister and mother."
~Mark 3:32-35

Family of birth
Family of choice
Walking the paths of life
Companions in the way.

Saturday

And when they could not bring him to Jesus because of the crowd, they removed the roof above him; and after having dug though it, they let down the mat on which the paralytic lay.
~Mark 2:4

Held by the chains of his life
The paralyzed one lies so still
Bound, unable to move in any direction
Friends yank him up and drop him at the feet of Jesus
Now pinned to his mat by the terror of possibility
Suddenly, released— he comes out— Dancing!!!

Proper 4: Sunday
Week of the Sunday closest to June 1

Even my best friend, whom I trusted,
who broke bread with me,
    has lifted up his heel and turned against me.
In my integrity you hold me fast,
    and shall set me before your face for ever.
~Psalm 41:9,12

light of integrity
illuminates the path
and keeps me from
the tangles of false trails.

Monday

237

By faith Moses, when he was grown up, refused to be called a son of Pharaoh's daughter, choosing rather to share ill-treatment with the people of God than to enjoy the fleeting pleasures of sin.
~Hebrews 11:24-25

Did some
sparks
from the burning bush
lodge in Moses'
heart?

Tuesday

"You search the scriptures because you think that in them you have eternal life, and it is they that testify on my behalf. Yet you refuse to come to me to have life.... But I know that you do not have the love of God in you."
~John 5:39-40,42

words and Word
one points to the other
but what a difference

we know H_2O
is the formula for water
but we KNOW water
drink after days
in dry deserts.

They will turn their faces upward, or they will look to the earth, but will see only distress and darkness, the gloom of anguish; and they will be thrust into thick darkness. But there will be no gloom for those who were in anguish.
~Isaiah 8:21b-9:1

Spinning into
dark and cold
the northern earth
turns from the sun
into the long night.
Stars blaze
from the universes
leading us on journeys
to stables of birth.

Thursday

Ah, you who make iniquitous decrees,
    who write oppressive statutes,
to turn aside the needy from justice
    and to rob the poor of my people of their right
that widows may be your spoil,
    and that you may make the orphans your prey!
What will you do on the day of punishment
    in the calamity that will come from far away?
To whom will you flee for help,
    and where will you leave your wealth
so as not to crouch among the prisoners
    or fall among the slain?
For all this his anger has not turned away;
    his hand is stretched out still.
~Isaiah 10:1-4

widows and orphans
the litmus test
of God's favor
life depends
on their song.

Friday

[Jesus said to Peter,] "Simon, Simon, listen! Satan has demanded to sift all of you like wheat, but I have prayed for you that your own faith may not fail; and you, when once you have turned back, strengthen your brothers." And he said to them, "Lord, I am ready to go with you to prison and to death!" Jesus said, "I tell you Peter, the cock will not crow this day, until you have denied three times that you know me."
~Luke 22:31-33

Tossed and shaken,
ground to flour.
Part of the bread making
but hard to see
from inside the oven.

Saturday

All human toil is for the mouth, yet the appetite is not satisfied.
~Ecclesiastes 6:7

For where your treasure is, there your heart will be also.
~Luke 12:34

Seeking without rest.
Sated yet not satisfied.
Searching futilely.
Pirate's gold will not buy joy.

"Ask, and it will be given you; search, and you will find; knock, and the door will be opened for you."
~Matthew 7:7

Maybe it should be---
Ask and a search will be given you.
Knock and doors will appear.

Monday

So I commend enjoyment, for there is nothing better for people under the sun than to eat, and drink, and enjoy themselves, for this will go with them in their toil through days of the life that God give them under the sun.
~Ecclesiastes 8:15

Squirrels of life
Store nuts of joy
to take out and savor
during long winters of toil.

Tuesday

For the whole law is summed up in a single commandment,
"You shall love your neighbor as yourself." If, however
you bite and devour one another, take care that you are
not consumed by one another.
~Galatians 5:14-15

Dragons of anger and hatred
blast forth from the heart
with consuming flames.
Where is the Water
to quench
this terrible fire?

Wednesday

Light is sweet, and it is pleasant for the eyes to see the sun. Even those who live many years should rejoice in them all; yet let them remember that the days of darkness will be many.

~Ecclesiastes 11:7-8

Blessing of sunrise
Greeting the dawn
Celebration of new day
A precious jewel
to delight the eyes
and offer hope
and possibilities.

Thursday

Save me, O God,
   for the waters have risen up to my neck.
I am sinking in deep mire,
   and there is no firm ground for my feet.
I have come into deep waters,
   and the torrent washes over me.
I have grown weary with my crying;
my throat is inflamed;
   my eyes have failed from looking for my God.
~Psalm 69:1-4

In the terror of the moment
I see only the mud and the waves.

Friday

The LORD is my shepherd;
    I shall not be in want.
~Psalm 23:1

In choosing to follow holiness
my deepest need
finds rest in green pastures
and still waters.

Saturday

Be my strong rock, a castle to keep me safe,
for you are my crag and my stronghold;
    for the sake of your Name, lead me and guide me.
~Psalm 31:3

Knights of the quest
need castles for rest.

Proper 6: Sunday
Week of the Sunday closest to June 15

For I am longing to see you so that I may share with you some spiritual gift to strengthen you— or rather so that we may be mutually encouraged by each other's faith, both yours and mine. I want you to know, brothers and sisters, that I have often intended to come to you (but thus far have been prevented), in order that I may reap some harvest among you as I have among the rest of the Gentiles. I am a debtor both to Greeks and to barbarians, both to the wise and to the foolish— hence my eagerness to proclaim the gospel to you also who are in Rome.

~Romans 1:11-15

In the teaching
is the learning.

The rabble among them had a strong craving; and the Israelites also wept again, and said, "If only we had meat to eat! We remember the fish we used to eat in Egypt for nothing, the cucumbers, the melons, the leeks, the onions, and the garlic; but now our strength is dried up, and there is nothing at all but this manna to look at."
~Numbers 11:4-6

The tongue tastes
the remembered richness
of forgotten slavery.

Tuesday

the disciples came to Jesus, saying, "Who is the greatest in the kingdom of heaven?" He called a child, whom he put among them, and said, "Truly I tell you, unless you change and become like children, you will never enter the kingdom of heaven."
~Matthew 18:1-4

Become like children?
Playing?
Dependent?
Tantrums?
Curious?
Wondering?
Delight?

So Miriam was shut out of the camp for seven days; and the people did not set out on the march until Miriam had been brought in again.
~Numbers 12:15

Moses-rescuer
Red Sea dancer
Punished with leprosy
by the law-writer.
But the journey is too hard
without the sound of her tambourine
so they wait.

Thursday

Peter came and said to Jesus, "LORD, if another member of the church sins against me, how often should I forgive? As many as seven times?" Jesus said to him, "Not seven times, but, I tell you, seventy-seven times."
~Matthew 18:21-22

Sometimes the offense
is so terrible
that it takes
7, 77, 777, 7777
or more
forgivings
to find peace.

Seven - the perfect number --
How many times will it take
for me to reach perfection
of forgiveness?

Friday

On the holy mountain stands the city he has founded;
    the LORD loves the gates of Zion
    more than all the dwellings of Jacob.
Glorious things are spoken of you,
    O city of our God.
I count Egypt and Babylon among those
    who know me;
    behold Philistia, Tyre, and Ethiopia:
    in Zion were they born.
Of Zion it shall be said, "Everyone was born in her,
    and the Most High himself shall sustain her."
The LORD will record as he enrolls the peoples,
    "These also were born there."
The singers and the dancers will say,
    "All my fresh springs are in you."
~Psalm 87:1-6

If we were all born in the City of God
Maybe we are suffering from sibling rivalry.

Saturday

"You know how to interpret the appearance of earth and sky, but why do you not know how to interpret the present time?"
~Luke 12:56

Where can we find the instruments
to predict
high and low pressure systems
dewpoints and rainfall
hurricanes and tornadoes
of our lives?
Where is our weather station?

Then someone came to him and said, "Teacher, what good deed must I do to have eternal life?" And he said to him, "Why do you ask me about what is good? There is only one who is good. If you wish to enter into life, keep the commandments. ... If you wish to be perfect, go, sell your possessions, and give the money to the poor, and you will have treasure in heaven; then come, follow me." When the young man heard this word, he went away grieving, for he had many possessions.
~Matthew 19:16-17, 21-22

Commandments:
tickets to the game.
But perfection
is a little more pricey.

Monday

"Again I tell you, it is easier for a camel to go through the eye of a needle than for someone who is rich to enter the kingdom of God."
~Matthew 19:24

Longingly looking
eye to eye
untangled and unknotted
stripped to its core
thread slips through the space
to be sewn into the fabric of life.

Tuesday

"When those hired about five o'clock came, each of them received the usual daily wage. Now when the first came, they thought they would receive more; but each of them also received the usual daily wage. And when they received it, they grumbled against the landowner, [who said] 'Am I not allowed to do what I choose with what belongs to me? Or are you envious because I am generous?' So the last will be first, and the first will be last."
~Matthew 20:9-11, 15-16

Chills of fear
run down the spines
of the first
when the last
receive generosity.

Wednesday

How beautiful upon the mountains
   are the feet of the messenger who
   announces peace,
who brings good news,
   who announces salvation.
~Isaiah 52:7

Flowers bloom
in the footsteps
of the peace-bearers.

Thursday

There were two blind men sitting by the roadside. When they heard that Jesus was passing by, they shouted, "Lᴏʀᴅ, have mercy on us, Son of David!" The crowd sternly ordered them to be quiet; but they shouted even more loudly, "Have mercy on us, Lᴏʀᴅ, Son of David!" Jesus stood still and called them, saying, "What do you want me to do for you?" ~Matthew 20:30-32

The crowd cannot see
the miracle in their midst
When do I let the crowd
silence me?
Allowing the moment of healing
to walk on?

Friday

What then are we to say? Should we continue in sin in order that grace may abound? By no means! How can we who died to sin go on living in it? Do you not know that all of us who have been baptized into Christ Jesus were baptized into his death? Therefore we have been buried with him by baptism into death, so that, just as Christ was raised from the dead by the glory of the Father, so we too might walk in newness of life.

For if we have been united with him in a death like his, we will certainly be united with him in a resurrection like his.
~Romans 6:1-5

Cross arcs across
the gap between
heaven and earth
holy and human
igniting
uniting.

She was bent over and was quite unable to stand up straight. When Jesus saw her, he called her over and said, "Woman, you are set free from your ailment." When he laid his hands on her, immediately she stood up straight and began praising God.
~Luke 13:11b-13

Seeing only
the dirt and rocks
of life
Bent with burdens

A touch
heals
frees
Suddenly straightening
Stretching
Seeing
Sun and stars
Friends and family
Dancing and singing on the way.

Proper 8: Sunday
Week of the Sunday closest to June 29

So Balaam rose in the morning, and said to the officials of Balak, "Go to your own land, for the LORD has refused to let me go with you." So the officials of Moab rose and went to Balak, and said, "Balaam refuses to come with us." Once again Balak sent officials, more numerous and more distinguished than these.
~Numbers 22:13-15

Pressure of power
seeks its way
Resistance comes
from centering
in the Holy One.

Monday

But now we are discharged from the law, dead to that which held us captive, so that we are slaves not under old written code but in the new life of the Spirit.
~Romans 7:6

Dead to old codes
Alive in the Spirit
Slaves of written word
or slaves in the new life
Do we miss our chains?
Do we wish for certainty?

Tuesday

When harvest time had come, he sent his slaves to the tenants to collect his produce. But the tenants seized his slaves and beat one, killed another, and stoned another.
~Matthew 21:34-35

When slave or son
asks for a share
of my harvest,
What will it be?
Stones or bread?

Wednesday

But I still my soul and make it quiet,
like a child upon its mother's breast;
my soul is quiet within me.
~Psalm 131:3

Warm, safe, easy
within a universe
of loving arms.
Making space for my soul.

Thursday

Deliver me, O LORD, from evildoers;
　　protect me from the violent,
Who devise evil in their hearts
　　and stir up strife all day long.
They have sharpened their tongues like a serpent;
　　adder's poison is under their lips.
Keep me, O LORD, from the hands of the wicked;
　　protect me from the violent,
　　who are determined to trip me up.
The proud have hidden a snare for me
and stretched out a net of cords;
　　they have set traps for me along the path.
I have said to the LORD, "You are my God;
　　listen, O LORD, to my supplication."
~Psalm 140:1-6

Pride must maintain
its lofty state
standing on top of the heap.

How shall we sing the Lord's song
   upon an alien soil?
If I forget you, O Jerusalem,
   let my right hand forget its skill.
Let my tongue cleave to the roof of my mouth
if I do not remember you,
   if I do not set Jerusalem above my highest joy.
Remember the day of Jerusalem, O Lord,
against the people of Edom,
   who said, "Down with it! down with it!
   even to the ground!"
O Daughter of Babylon, doomed to destruction,
   happy the one who pays you back
   for what you have done to us!
Happy shall he be who takes your little ones,
   and dashes them against the rock!
~Psalm 137:4-9

The pain of exile
gives rise to revenge
Is there another way?

Saturday

Light shines in the darkness for the upright;
>   the righteous are merciful and full of compassion
It is good for them to be generous in lending
>   and to manage their affairs with justice.
For they will never be shaken;
>   the righteous will be kept in everlasting
>   remembrance.
They will not be afraid of any evil rumors;
>   their heart is right;
>   they put their trust in the LORD
Their heart is established and will not shrink,
>   until they see their desire upon their enemies.
They have given freely to the poor,
>   and their righteousness stands fast for ever;
>   they will hold up their head with honor.
The wicked will see it and be angry;
they will gnash their teeth and pine away;
>   The desires of the wicked will perish.
~Psalm 112:4-10

Toothless enemies
Evoke no fear
Only laughter
And pity.

Proper 9: Sunday
Week of the Sunday closest to July 6

Happy are they who have not walked in the counsel of
    the wicked,
    nor lingered in the way of sinners,
    nor sat in the seats of the scornful!
Their delight is in the law of the LORD,
    and they meditate on his law day and night.
They are like trees planted by streams of water,
bearing fruit in due season,
    with leaves that do not wither;
    everything they do shall prosper.
It is not so with the wicked;
    they are like chaff which the wind blows away.
Therefore the wicked shall not stand upright
    when judgment comes,
    nor the sinner in the council of the righteous.
For the LORD knows the way of the righteous,
    but the way of the wicked is doomed.
~Psalm 1:1-6

Roots of my tree
extend into the source
fed by prayer, rest, and work.

Monday: St. Benedict

Give ear to my words, O LORD;
    consider my meditation.
Hearken to my cry for help, my King and my God,
    for I make my prayer to you.
In the morning, LORD, you hear my voice;
    early in the morning I make my appeal and watch
        for you.
~Psalm 5: 1-3

A psalm for
followers of
all traditions
who rise to greet
the day
with prayer.

Tuesday

"Choose for each of your tribes individuals who are wise, discerning, and reputable to be your leaders." You answered me, "The plan you have proposed is a good one." So I took the leaders of your tribes, wise and reputable individuals, and installed them as leaders over you, commanders of thousands, commanders of hundreds, commanders of fifties, commanders of tens, and officials, throughout your tribes. I charged your judges at that time: "Give the members of your community a fair hearing, and judge rightly between one person and another, whether citizen or resident alien. You must not be partial in judging: hear out the small and the great alike; you shall not be intimidated by anyone, for the judgment is God's."
~Deuteronomy 1:13-17a

Wise and impartial judges
the hope of all societies.

Wednesday

Always be ready to make your defense to anyone who demands from you an accounting for the hope that is in you; yet do it with gentleness and reverence.
~1 Peter 3:15b-16a

The IRS agents of life
are auditing your accounts.
How did you come up
with so much hope?
Was it ordinary income
or a gift?

O Lord, you are my portion and my cup;
　　it is You who uphold my lot.
My boundaries enclose a pleasant land;
　　indeed, I have a goodly heritage.
I will bless the Lord who gives me counsel;
　　my heart teaches me, night after night.
I have set the Lord always before me;
　　because You are at my right hand I shall not fall.
~Psalm 16:5-8

Boundaries
of holiness
provide safety
for the soul.

Friday

Some put their trust in chariots and some in horses,
    but we will call upon the Name of the
    LORD our God.
They collapse and fall down,
    but we will arise and stand upright.
O LORD, give victory to the king
    and answer us when we call.
~Psalm 20:7-9

A name more powerful
than chariots and horses
tanks and guns?
Willing to die
instead of calling upon
armies of angels?

Saturday

"As I was with Moses, so I will be with you; I will not fail you or forsake you. Be strong and courageous; for you shall put this people in possession of the land that I swore to their ancestors to give them. Only be strong and very courageous."
~Joshua 1:5b

What land of promise
are we seeking?
How easily
we fade
and lose heart.
Be strong.
Be courageous.

Joshua son of Nun sent two men secretly from Shittim as spies, saying, "Go, view the land, especially Jericho." So they went, and entered the house of a prostitute whose name was Rahab, and spent the night there.
~Joshua 2:1

Rahab
Ancestor of Jesus
Woman of mystery
protector and provider
for family and foe.
Tell us your story.

"But the one who had received the one talent went off and dug a hole in the ground and hid his master's money."
~Matthew 25:18

Who
are the coins
buried and waiting
to be spent?

Tuesday

As regards the gospel they are enemies of God for your sake; but as regards election they are beloved, for the sake of their ancestors; for the gifts and the calling of God are irrevocable.
~Romans 11:28-29

Beloved enemies
Lives intertwined
with ours
grows strange and wondrous fruit.

Wednesday

Do not be conformed to this world, but be transformed by the renewing of your minds, so that you may discern what is the will of God— what is good and acceptable and perfect.

For by the grace given to me I say to everyone among you not to think of yourself more highly than you ought to think, but to think with sober judgment, each according to the measure of faith that God has assigned. For as in one body we have many members, and not all the members have the same function, so we, who are many, are one body in Christ, and individually we are members one of another.
~Romans 12:2-5

many
increase
possibilities
of perfection.

Thursday

If it is possible, so far as it depends on you, live peaceably with all. Beloved, never avenge yourselves, but leave room for the wrath of God; for it is written, "Vengeance is mine, I will repay, says the LORD." No, "if your enemies are hungry, feed them; if they are thirsty, give them something to drink; for by doing this you will heap burning coals on their heads." Do not be overcome by evil, but overcome evil with good.
~Romans 12:18-21

Cleansing waves
sweep the beaches
free of litter.

Friday

Peter said to him, "Though all become deserters because of you, I will never desert you." Jesus said to him, "Truly I tell you, this very night, before the cock crows, you will deny me three times." Peter said to him, "Even though I must die with you, I will not deny you." And so said all the disciples.

~Matthew 26:33-35

A gap occurs
between promise
and action.
Our thoughts
cannot spark deeds.

Saturday

Then the angel showed me the river of the water of life, bright as crystal, flowing from the throne of God and of the Lamb through the middle of the street of the city. On either side of the river is the tree of life with its twelve kinds of fruit, producing its fruit each month; and the leaves of the tree are for the healing of the nations.
~ Revelations 22:1-2

Leaves steeping
in the pot
Cups and mugs
awaiting those
who would drink
the infusion of healing and peace.
A tea party for the nations.

Proper 11: Sunday
Week of the Sunday closest to July 20

Then he said to them, "I am deeply grieved, even to death; remain here, and stay awake with me." And going a little farther, he threw himself on the ground and prayed, "My Father, if it is possible, let this cup pass from me; yet not what I want but what you want." Then he came to the disciples and found them sleeping; and he said to Peter, "So, could you not stay awake with me one hour? Stay awake and pray that you may not come into the time of trial; the spirit indeed is willing, but the flesh is weak." Again he went away for the second time and prayed, "My Father, if this cannot pass unless I drink it, your will be done." Again he came and found them sleeping, for their eyes were heavy. So leaving them again, he went away and prayed for the third time, saying the same words. Then he came to the disciples and said to them, "Are you still sleeping and taking your rest?"
~Matthew 26:38-45a

Escape
in sleep
from images
too painful to see.

Monday

Welcome those who are weak in faith, but not for the purpose of quarreling over opinions. Some believe in eating anything, while the weak eat only vegetables. Those who eat must not despise those who abstain, and those who abstain must not pass judgment on those who eat; for God has welcomed them. Who are you to pass judgment on servants of another? It is before their own lord that they stand or fall. And they will be upheld, for the LORD is able to make them stand.
~Romans 14:1-4

Embraced by holiness
Souls expand
Hearts speak.

Tuesday

Then the high priest tore his clothes and said, "He has blasphemed!"
~Matthew 26:65

Clothing torn
Curtain in the temple torn
Minds and hearts torn
Is it blasphemy
or the Word of God?

Wedensday

The LORD, the God of gods, has spoken;
  he has called the earth from the rising of the sun
    to its setting.
Out of Zion, perfect in its beauty,
  God reveals himself in glory.
Our God will come and will not keep silence;
  before him there is a consuming flame,
  and round about him a raging storm.
He calls the heavens and the earth from above
  to witness the judgment of his people.
~Psalm 50:1-4

Wrapped in storms
Raging, flame-throwing
Judgment comes burning
through our shame
stripping the burdens of the years
freeing us to join the dance
of heavens and earth.

Thursday

When Judas, his betrayer, saw that Jesus was condemned, he repented and brought back the thirty pieces of silver to the chief priests and the elders. He said, "I have sinned by betraying innocent blood." But they said, "What is that to us? See to it yourself." Throwing down the pieces of silver in the temple, he departed; and he went and hanged himself.
~Matthew 27:3-5

Sometimes the tasks
we are given
are too hard to bear.

Friday

My companion stretched forth his hand against
        his comrade;
    he has broken his covenant.
His speech is softer than butter,
    but war is in his heart.
His words are smoother than oil,
    but they are drawn swords.
Cast your burden upon the LORD,
and he will sustain you;
    he will never let the righteous stumble.
For you will bring the bloodthirsty and deceitful
    down to the pit of destruction, O God.
They shall not live out half their days,
    but I will put my trust in you.
~Psalm 55:21-26

Hard to trust
when trust
is broken.

Saturday

Some were convinced by what he had said, while others
refused to believe.
~Acts 28:24

talking
talking
talking
when words can not convince
seeing creates believing.

Proper 12: Sunday
Week of the Sunday closest to July 27

The bones of Joseph, which the Israelites had brought up from Egypt, were buried at Shechem, in the portion of ground that Jacob had bought from the children of Hamor, the father of Shechem, for one hundred pieces of money; it became an inheritance of the descendants of Joseph.
~Joshua 24:32

All those years
of carrying Joseph's bones.
Finally at rest.
What memories do I carry
that need burying?

Monday

As they went out, they came upon a man from Cyrene named Simon; they compelled this man to carry his cross.
~Matthew 27:32

Swept up
in the events
of the day
Shoulders of strangers
carry burdens
not chosen.

Tuesday

From noon on, darkness came over the whole land until three in the afternoon. And about three o'clock Jesus cried with a loud voice, "Eli, Eli, lema sabachthani?" that is, "My God, my God, why have you forsaken me?" When some of the bystanders heard it, they said, "This man is calling for Elijah."
~Matthew 27:45-47

Both the sky and the Man
were full of clouds
on that day.

When it was evening, there came a rich man from Arimathea, named Joseph, who was also a disciple of Jesus. He went to Pilate and asked for the body of Jesus; then Pilate ordered it to be given to him. So Joseph took the body and wrapped it in a clean linen cloth and laid it in his own new tomb, which he had hewn in the rock. He then rolled a great stone to the door of the tomb and went away. Mary Magdalene and the other Mary were there, sitting opposite the tomb.
~Matthew 27:57-61

Another Joseph
wrapping Jesus
in swaddling clothes
Rich man
knows his poverty.

Thursday

"this is what was spoken through the prophet Joel:
'In the last days it will be, God declares,
that I will pour out my spirit upon all flesh,
    and your sons and your daughters shall prophesy,
and your young men shall see visions,
    and your old men shall dream dreams.
Even upon my slaves, both men and women,
    in those days I will pour out my Spirit;
    and they shall prophesy.'"
~Acts 2:16-18

Signs of the times:
when all are free
to speak
to dream
to prophesy.

Friday

I fell down to worship at the feet of the angel who showed them to me; but he said to me, "You must not do that! I am a fellow servant with you."
~Revelation 22:8b-9a

It is hard
Not
to fall at the feet
of an angel.

Saturday

The crowd came together again, so that [Jesus and his disciples] could not even eat. When his family heard it, they went out to restrain him, for people were saying, "He has gone out of his mind."
~Mark 3:20-21

Frantic family rides
to the rescue
with home cooking.

So Gideon took ten of his servants, and did as the L ORD
had told him; but because he was too afraid of his family
and townspeople to do it by day, he did it by night.
~Judges 6:27

Obedient but
not quite
Willing but
fearful
"What will people think"
holds hearts hostage.

Monday

[John] said,
> "I am the voice of the one crying out
>> in the wilderness,
> 'Make straight the way of the LORD,'"
as the prophet Isaiah said.
~John 1:23

Clear the way
remove the briars
pry out the stones
fill in the potholes.
Make the path
to our hearts
open to this guest.

Tuesday

When Jesus turned and saw them following, he said to them, "What are you looking for?" They said to him, "Rabbi"(which translated means Teacher), "Where are you staying?" He said to them, "Come and see."
~John 1:38-39

Hearts or houses
Tents or temples
Where is the Teacher staying?
Is there a spare room in our home?

Wednesday

My mouth shall speak the praise of the LORD;
    let all flesh bless his holy Name for ever and ever.
~Psalm 145:22

Words are only the beginning of praise.

Thursday

Jesus did this, the first of his signs, in Cana of Galilee, and revealed his glory; and his disciples believed in him.

~John 2:11

Step by step
we open ourselves
to a wondrous
reality.

Friday

In the temple he found people selling cattle, sheep, and doves, and the money changers seated at their tables. Making a whip of cords, he drove all of them out of the temple, both the sheep and the cattle. He also poured out the coins of the money changers and overturned their tables.
~John 2:13-15

Turning over
the tables
of the calculating mind
Loosening the grip
of the clenched
and grasping hand
Open to
the generosity
of the Source.

So there arose an Israelite custom that for four days every year the daughters of Israel would go out to lament the daughter of Jephthah the Gileadite.
~Judges 11:39b-40

Weeping and mourning
for the lost daughter
and all her sisters
throughout the ages.

Proper 14: Sunday
Week of the Sunday closest to August 10

Righteousness and justice are the
foundations of your throne;
    love and truth go before your face.
Happy are the people who know the festal shout!
    they walk, O LORD, in the light of your presence.
~Psalm 89:14-15

Rah, rah, rah
Sis-boom-bah
Yay
Whoopee
Hip, hip, hooray
Awesome
ai-eee
Hurrah
Hosanna

Skip, leap, shout
around the throne of justice and righteousness
What a victory dance that will be.

Monday

But a Pharisee in the council named Gamaliel, a teacher of the law, respected by all the people, stood up and ordered the men to be put outside for a short time. Then he said to them, "Fellow Israelites, consider carefully what you propose to do to these men. ... So in the present case, I tell you, keep away from these men and let them alone; because if this plan or this undertaking is of human origin, it will fail; but if it is of God, you will not be able to overthrow them— in that case you may even be found fighting against God!"
~Acts 5:34-35,38-39

Proof of God's presence
plays out in persistence.

Tuesday

"For what will it profit them if they gain the whole world but forfeit their life?"
~Matthew 16:26a

Life is in the playing.
We will never
get into the game
if we sit on the bench
or stay safe
and take a forfeit.

Wednesday

He sent a man before them,
    Joseph, who was sold as a slave.
They bruised his feet in fetters;
    his neck they put in an iron collar.
Until his prediction came to pass,
    the word of the LORD tested him.
The king sent and released him;
    the ruler of the peoples set him free.
He set him as a master over his household,
    as a ruler over all his possessions,
To instruct his princes according to his will
    and to teach his elders wisdom.
~ Psalm 105:17-22

Fetters and chains
bind the body
While minds can wander
over the wideness of wisdom.

Thursday

So they read from the book, from the law of God, with interpretation. They gave the sense, so that the people understood the reading. And Nehemiah, who was the governor, and Ezra the priest and scribe, and the Levites who taught the people said to all the people, "This day is holy to the LORD your God; do not mourn or weep." For all the people wept when they heard the words of the law. Then he said to them, "Go your way, eat the fat and drink sweet wine and send portions of them to those for whom nothing is prepared, for this day is holy to our LORD; and do not be grieved, for the joy of the LORD is your strength."
~Nehemiah 8:8-10

The muddy waters
cleared in droplets of understanding
Tears turning to joy
at the clarity of it all.

Friday

The sick man answered him, "Sir, I have no one to put me into the pool when the water is stirred up; and while I am making my way, someone else steps down ahead of me."
~John 5:7

In the stirring
is the healing.

"The kingdom of heaven is like a mustard seed....
The kingdom of heaven is like yeast."
~Matthew 13:31, 33

Tiny grains
placed in the mix
can change the world.

Proper 15: Sunday
Week of the Sunday closest to August 17

"And can any of you by worrying add a single hour to your span of life?"
~Luke 12:2

Picking and pulling
at the threads
of my life
I worry it to shreds.
The weaver of days
Lovingly
gathers the pieces and
knits me back together.

Monday

Pray for the peace of Jerusalem:
  "May they prosper who love you.
Peace be within your walls
  and quietness within your towers.
For my brethren and companions' sake,
  I pray for your prosperity.
Because of the house of the LORD our God,
  I will seek to do you good."
~Psalm 122:6-9

If the whole world prays
will they cease their warring ways?
Where is the peace within the walls of our hearts
or quietness in the towers of our minds?

Tuesday

"Where did this man get this wisdom and these deeds of power? Is not this the carpenter's son? Is not his mother called Mary? And are not his brothers James and Joseph and Simon and Judas? And are not all his sisters with us? Where then did this man get all this?"
~Matthew 13:54b-56a

Looking to
magical outsiders
for wisdom and power
We miss the knowledge of our own hearts.

Wednesday

I lie in the midst of lions that devour the people;
    their teeth are spears and arrows,
    their tongue a sharp sword.
They have laid a net for my feet,
and I am bowed low;
    they have dug a pit before me,
    but have fallen into it themselves.
Exalt yourself above the heavens, O God,
    and your glory over all the earth.
My heart is firmly fixed, O God, my heart is fixed;
    I will sing and make melody.
~Psalm 57:4-7

When the terrible teeth
cage my days
My song escapes
to claim the space.

Thursday

Hear my cry, O God,
    and listen to my prayer.
I call upon you from the ends of the earth
with heaviness in my heart;
    set me upon the rock that is higher than I.
For you have been my refuge,
    a strong tower against the enemy.
~Psalm 61:1-3

Surrounded by God-walls
Stronger than stone
Higher than heaven
I rest from my fears.

Friday

"In your great mercy, O God,
    answer me with your unfailing help.
Save me from the mire; do not let me sink;
    let me be rescued from those who hate me
    and out of the deep waters.
Let not the torrent of waters wash over me,
neither let the deep swallow me up;
    do not let the Pit shut its mouth upon me.
Answer me, O LORD, for your love is kind;
    in your great compassion, turn to me."
~Psalm 69:15-18

Drowning in the depths
of despair
The Pit of apathy
threatens hope.

Saturday

When Jesus came to the leader's house and saw the flute players and the crowd making a commotion, he said, "Go away; for the girl is not dead but sleeping." And they laughed at him. But when the crowd had been put outside, he went in and took her by the hand, and the girl got up.
~Matthew 9:23-25

Pushing past
the walls of laughter
Reaching a hand
into the cave of death
The Jokester pulls a girl
out of the undertaker's hat.

Proper 16: Sunday
Week of the Sunday closest to August 24

"Truly I tell you, among those born of women not one has arisen greater than John the Baptist; yet the least in the kingdom of heaven is greater than he."
~Matthew 11:11

Standing on the edges
Unnoticed and small
The team Captain hands you a uniform
With your name embroidered on the back
Chosen for the team of life.

Monday

"It is like children sitting in the marketplaces and calling
to one another,
    'We piped to you, and you did not dance;
        we wailed, and you did not mourn.'"
~Matthew 11:16-17

Fitfulness of the soul
A temper tantrum in my spirit
A sleepless night of restless dreams.
Nothing satisfies
as I sit with "remote" in hand
switching channels on my life.

Tuesday

"Therefore my beloved, be steadfast, immovable, always excelling in the work of the LORD, because you know that in the LORD your labor is not in vain."
~1 Corinthians 15:58

Each piece of the puzzle
Has a place
In the grand design.

Wednesday

"And who is my neighbor?"
~Luke 10:b

Who will be neighbor to me?
Lying in the ditches of life
Fine words and pure rituals
cannot touch the bruises
of my being.

Thursday

who alone stretched out the heavens
    and trampled the waves of the Sea;
who made the Bear and Orion,
    the Pleiades and the chambers of the south;
who does great things beyond understanding,
    and marvelous things without number.
~Job 9:8-10

Icy constellations
process in starry array.
The clouds part
and hearts connect
across the continents and seas.

Friday

Job answered:
"I loathe my life;
I will give free utterance to my complaint;
I will speak in the bitterness of my soul.
I will say to God, Do not condemn me;
    let me know why you contend against me.
Does it seem good to you to oppress,
    to despise the work of your hands
    and favor the schemes of the wicked?"
~Job 9:1, 10:1-3

Logic of life
subtracts joy
and adds up to
bitterness of soul
When suffering
multiplies and
divides us.

Saturday

Who turned the hard rock into a pool of water
and flint-stone into a flowing spring.
~Psalm 114:8

Unlikely sources
quench the thirst of souls.

The disciples determined that according to their ability, each would send relief to the believers living in Judea; this they did, sending it to the elders by Barnabas and Saul.
~Acts 11:29-30

Faith overcomes fear
Abundance appears
in the midst of scarcity.

Monday

"If you would only keep silent,
    that would be your wisdom!"
~Job 13:5

Tangles of words
wash up on the
beaches of our souls
Will one pearl be found
in a silent shell?

Tuesday

Incline my heart to your decrees
    and not to unjust gain.
Turn my eyes from watching what is worthless;
    give me life in your ways.
~Psalm 119:36-37

Vision forms action.
Look upon holiness
to nurture life.

Wednesday

Now it was the sabbath day when Jesus made the mud
and opened his eyes.
~John 9:14

Created from mud
on the sixth day
our eyes are opened on the seventh???

They answered him, "You were born entirely in sins, and are you trying to teach us?" And they drove him out.
~John 9:34

Teachers
often
have difficulty
being taught.
It is hard to learn
when one has all the answers.

Friday

"Whoever enters by me will be saved, and will come in and go out and find pasture."
~John 10:9b

Without freedom
to come and go
we starve.

Saturday

Then [Jesus] began to speak and taught them, saying: "You are the salt of the earth; but if salt has lost its taste, how can its saltiness be restored? It is no longer good for anything, but is thrown out and trampled under foot." ~Matthew 5:2,13

Salt filled birthwaters
Ebb away in blandness.
Tears and sweat bring out the salt again.

Proper 18: Sunday
Week of the Sunday closest to September 7

At that time the festival of the Dedication took place in Jerusalem. It was winter and Jesus was walking in the temple, in the portico of Solomon.
~John 10:22-23

Festival of Dedication
Hanukkah
Season of joy,
of restoration,
from desecration.
One by one the candles
illuminate
and we see.

When the crowds saw what Paul had done, they shouted in the Lycaonian language, "The gods have come down to us in human form!" Barnabas they called Zeus, and Paul they called Hermes, because he was the chief speaker ... "Friends, why are you doing this? We are mortals just like you, and bring you good news, that you should turn from these worthless things to the living God, who made the heaven and the earth and the sea, and all that is in them."
~Acts 14:11-12, 15

Putting leaders
on pedestals
for worship.
Smashing pedestals
for stones
to destroy them.
Acclaiming and blaming
in our endless
restless
search for idols.

Tuesday

Thomas, who was called the Twin, said to his fellow disciples, "Let us also go, that we may die with him."
~John 11:16

No doubts today
for Thomas.

Now Bethany was near Jerusalem, some two miles away, and many of the Jews had come to Martha and Mary to console them about their brother.
~John 11:18-19

Gatherings of gladness
and celebration
of conversation and bread broken
Now a place of sadness
and mourning
of silence and emptiness
Circle of friends
grieving the loss of brother and companion.

Thursday

When he had said this, he cried with a loud voice, "Lazarus, come out!" The dead man came out, his hands and face bound with strips of cloth, and his face wrapped in a cloth. Jesus said to them, "Unbind him, and let him go."
~John 11:43-44

In the depths of the earth
I hear my name
spoken with life
called back to community
Freed by a Word.

Friday

For had it been an adversary who taunted me,
then I could have borne it;
    or had it been an enemy who vaunted himself
        against me,
    then I could have hidden from him,
But it was you, a man after my own heart,
    my companion, my own familiar friend.
We took sweet counsel together,
    and walked with the throng in the house of God.
~Psalm 55:13-15

Knife to the heart
from the hand of a friend
leaves a wound
that will not heal.

Saturday

"So when you are offering your gift at the altar, if you remember that your brother or sister has something against you, leave your gift there before the altar, and go; first be reconciled to your brother or sister, and then come and offer your gift."
~Matthew 5:23-24

Gifts are worthless
when relationships
have no value.

Proper 19: Sunday
Week of the Sunday closest to September 14

Paul wanted Timothy to accompany him; and he took him and had him circumcised because of the Jews who were in those places, for they all knew that his father was a Greek.
~Acts 15:36-16:5

Paul gives in to peer pressure?
or opens the way for the future?
Do I know my reasons
for going along with the crowd?

Monday

On the sabbath day we went outside the gate by the river, where we supposed there was a place of prayer; and we sat down and spoke to the women who had gathered there. A certain woman named Lydia, a worshipper of God, was listening to us; she was from the city of Thyatira and a dealer in purple cloth. The LORD opened her heart to listen eagerly to what was said by Paul. When she and her household were baptized, she urged us, saying, "If you have judged me to be faithful to the LORD, come and stay at my home." And she prevailed upon us.

~Acts 16:13-15

Lydia, dealer in purple cloth
successful business woman
head of household
Sits by the river
listening
What did Paul say
that caused this certain woman
to become so certain?

Tuesday

The LORD blessed the latter days of Job more than his beginning; and he had fourteen thousand sheep, six thousand camels, a thousand yoke of oxen, and a thousand donkeys. He also had seven sons and three daughters. He named the first Jemimah, the second Keziah, and the third Keren-happuch. In all the land there were no women so beautiful as Job's daughters; and their father gave them an inheritance along with their brothers.

~Job 42:12-15

Daughters with names and an inheritance
Amazing.
Debating with God has its benefits.

Wednesday

Yours is the day, yours also the night;
   you established the moon and the sun.
You fixed the boundaries of the earth;
   you made both summer and winter.
Do not hand over the life of your dove to wild beasts;
   never forget the lives of your poor.
Let not the oppressed turn away ashamed;
   let the poor and needy praise your Name.
~Psalm 74:15-16, 18, 20

Night and day
Summer and winter
Chaos of poverty and oppression
Profane the holiness of the creation.

Thursday

Nevertheless many, even of the authorities, believed in him. But because of the Pharisees they did not confess it, for fear that they would be put out of the synagogue; for they loved human glory more than the glory that comes from God.
~John 12:42-43

Fear closes
doors
in all directions.

Friday

While Paul was waiting for them in Athens, he was deeply distressed to see that the city was full of idols. So he argued in the synagogue with the Jews and the devout persons, and also in the marketplace every day with those who happened to be there. Also some Epicurean and Stoic philosophers debated with him. Some said, "What does this babbler want to say?" Others said, "He seems to be a proclaimer of foreign divinities." (This was because he was telling the good news about Jesus and the resurrection.) So they took him and brought him to the Areopagus and asked him, "May we know what this new teaching is that you are presenting? It sounds rather strange to us, so we would like to know what it means." Now all the Athenians and the foreigners living there would spend their time in nothing but telling or hearing something new.
~Acts 17:16-21

Idlers having an idyll,
idly wondering
among the idols.

The waters have lifted up, O LORD,
the waters have lifted up their voice;
    the waters have lifted up their pounding waves.
Mightier than the sound of many waters,
mightier than the breakers of the sea,
    mightier is the LORD who dwells on high.
~Psalm 93:4-5

Like a fish
longing for the seas
when cast up
on the beach
dry and gasping
for water,
I yearn for the ease
of days of certainty.

Proper 20: Sunday
Week of the Sunday closet to September 21

Restore us, O God of hosts;
　　show the light of your countenance,
　　and we shall be saved.
O LORD God of hosts,
　　how long will you be angered
　　despite the prayers of your people?
You have fed them with the bread of tears;
　　you have given them bowls of tears to drink.
~Psalm 80:3-5

Did Lot's wife
eat this bread
and drink from this bowl
until she turned into a pillar of salt?

Monday

Then he sent and called for his friends and his wife Zeresh, and Haman recounted to them the splendor of his riches, the number of his sons, all the promotions with which the king had honored him, and how he had advanced him above the officials and the ministers of the king. Haman added, "Even Queen Esther let no one but myself come with the king to the banquet that she prepared. Tomorrow also I am invited by her, together with the king. Yet all this does me no good so long as I see the Jew Mordecai sitting at the king's gate." Then his wife Zeresh and all his friends said to him, "Let a gallows fifty cubits high be made, and in the morning tell the king to have Mordecai hanged on it; then go with the king to the banquet in good spirits." This advice pleased Haman, and he had the gallows made.
~Esther 5:10b-14

A rope of hate
braided for the gallows
The noose tightens
on the days of power.

Tuesday

Jesus, full of the Holy Spirit, returned from the Jordan and was led by the Spirit in the wilderness, where for forty days he was tempted by the devil. He ate nothing at all during those days, and when they were over, he was famished.... When the devil had finished every test, he departed from him until an opportune time.
~Luke 4:1-2,13

Hungry
Angry
Lonely
Tired
The opportune times for temptation.

Truly, his salvation is very near to those
     who fear him,
  that his glory may dwell in our land.
Mercy and truth have met together;
  righteousness and peace have kissed each other.
~Psalm 85:9-10

Entwined on a balance point
in a lover's embrace
Mercy and truth
Righteousness and peace
Merge into union
For the salvation of all.

Thursday

He went down to Capernaum, a city in Galilee, and was teaching them on the sabbath. They were astounded at his teaching, because he spoke with authority. In the synagogue there was a man who had the spirit of an unclean demon, and he cried out with a loud voice, "Let us alone! What have you to do with us, Jesus of Nazareth? Have you come to destroy us? I know who you are, the Holy One of God." But Jesus rebuked him, saying, "Be silent, and come out of him!" When the demon had thrown him down before them, he came out of him without having done him any harm. They were all amazed and kept saying to one another, "What kind of utterance is this? For with authority and power he commands the unclean spirits, and out they come!" And a report about him began to reach every place in the region.
~Luke 4:31-37

Tornadoes and dust devils
cannot disturb the One
who is truly grounded.

Demons also came out of many, shouting, "You are the Son of God!" But he rebuked them and would not allow them to speak, because they knew he was the Messiah.
~Luke 4:41

Disintegration
recognizes
integration
and can not be still.

Saturday

How great a forest is set ablaze by a small fire! And the tongue is a fire.
~James 3:5b-6a

The fire extinguisher
hangs in the hallway
between the ears and the heart.

When he had finished speaking, he knelt down with them all and prayed. There was much weeping among them all; they embraced Paul and kissed him, grieving especially because of what he had said, that they would not see him again.
~Acts 20:17-38

The unspoken words
at each parting are
"We may never see one another again."

Monday

Just then some men came, carrying a paralyzed man on a bed. They were trying to bring him in and lay him before Jesus; but finding no way to bring him in because of the crowd, they went up on the roof and let him down in front of Jesus.
~Luke 5:18-19

Who needs
carrying to Jesus?
Where do we
need to break the roof?
Tear down the walls?
Where are the crowds
blocking the way?
Do we know
the paralyzed ones of today?

Tuesday

I will not punish your daughters
       when they play the whore,
    nor your daughters-in-law
           when they commit adultery;
for the men themselves go aside with whores,
    and sacrifice with temple prostitutes;
thus a people without understanding come to ruin.
~Hosea 4:14

Those who
can choose
must bear the
punishment.

Wednesday

On another sabbath he entered the synagogue and taught, and there was a man there whose right hand was withered. The scribes and the Pharisees watched him to see whether he would cure on the sabbath, so that they might find an accusation against him. Even though he knew what they were thinking, he said to the man who had the withered hand, "Come and stand here." He got up and stood there. Then Jesus said to them, "I ask you, is it lawful to do good or to do harm on the sabbath, to save life or to destroy it?" After looking around at all of them, he said to him, "Stretch out your hand." He did so, and his hand was restored. But they were filled with fury and discussed with one another what they might do to Jesus.

~Luke 6:6-11

One withered hand
restored
Many hearts wither.

Thursday

"Blessed are you who are poor,
        for yours is the kingdom of God.
    Blessed are you who are hungry now,
        for you will be filled.
    Blessed are you who weep now,
        for you will laugh.
Blessed are you when people hate you, when they
exclude you, revile you, and defame you on account of
the Son of Man. Rejoice in that day and leap for joy,
for surely your reward is great in heaven; for that is
what their ancestors did to the prophets.
    But woe to you who are rich,
        for you have received your consolation.
    Woe to you who are full now,
        for you will be hungry.
    Woe to you who are laughing now,
        for you will mourn and weep.
    Woe to you when all speak well of you, for that is
what their ancestors did to the false prophets."
~Luke 6:20-26

Rich, full
happy, adored
Woeful?
Poor, hungry
weeping, reviled
Blessed?
What an odd universe.

Friday

"Do not judge, and you will not be judged; do not condemn, and you will not be condemned. Forgive, and you will be forgiven; give, and it will be given to you. A good measure, pressed down, shaken together, running over, will be put into your lap; for the measure you give will be the measure you get back."
~Luke 6:37-38

The flour of forgiveness
Ground in generosity
Sifted free of stones.

Saturday

For this I will lament and wail;
I will go barefoot and naked;
I will make lamentation like the jackals,
and mourning like the ostriches.
~Micah 1:8

Wandering
in the wilderness of loss
the Holy mourns
separation.

Proper 22: Sunday
Week of the Sunday closest to October 5

Happy are those who act with justice
    and always do what is right!
Remember me, O LORD, with the favor you have
        for your people,
    and visit me with your saving help;
That I may see the prosperity of your elect
and be glad with the gladness of your people,
    that I may glory with your inheritance.
~Psalm 106:3-5

Justice in community
is the salvation of each
A world of gladness
is the glory for each.

Now the son of Paul's sister heard about the ambush; so he went and gained entrance to the barracks and told Paul.
~Acts 23:16

Somehow one
never thinks of Paul
with a sister
and a nephew.
Was she his little sister
Or big sister?
Even saints have families.

Tuesday

Alas for those who devise wickedness
    and evil deeds on their beds!
When the morning dawns, they perform it,
    because it is in their power.
~Micah 2:1

Early in the morning I cry out to you,
    for in your word is my trust.
My eyes are open in the night watches,
    that I may meditate upon your promise.
~Psalm 119:147-148

Deeds of wickedness
Deeds of promise
Dreamt in the night
The morning waits in expectation.

Wednesday

"I have a hope in God— a hope that they themselves also accept— that there will be a resurrection of both the righteous and the unrighteous."
~Acts 24:15

Bouquets
of weeds
and roses
will be picked
for the Banquet Table.

Thursday

[God] shall judge between many peoples,
    and shall arbitrate between
        strong nations far away;
they shall beat their swords into plowshares,
    and their spears into pruning hooks;
nation shall not lift up sword against nation,
    neither shall they learn war any more;
but they shall all sit under their
        own vines and under their
        own fig trees,
    and no one shall make them afraid;
    for the mouth of the LORD of hosts has spoken.
~Micah 4:3-4

Now we are beating
the plowshares into swords
and pruning hooks into spears
They want to sit under others' trees
and fear rules the world.
No one listens.

Friday

"No one after lighting a lamp hides it under a jar, or puts it under a bed, but puts it on a lampstand, so that those who enter may see the light. For nothing is hidden that will not be disclosed, nor is anything secret that will not become known and come to light. Then pay attention to how you listen; for to those who have, more will be given; and from those who do not have, even what they seem to have will be taken away."
~Luke 8:16-18

Open hands and hearts
receive gifts
Closed fists lose all.

Saturday

"O my people, what have I done to you?
In what have I wearied you? Answer me!
For I brought you up from the land of Egypt,
and redeemed you from the house of slavery;
and I sent before you Moses, Aaron, and Miriam."
~Micah 6:3-4

Saving deeds
Leaders of the promise
Forgotten history
in the riches
and greed
of the day.

Jesus then asked him, "What is your name?" He said, "Legion"; for many demons had entered him. They begged him not to order them to go back into the abyss.

Now there on the hillside a large herd of swine was feeding; and the demons begged Jesus to let them enter these. So he gave them permission. Then the demons came out of the man and entered the swine, and the herd rushed down the steep bank into the lake and was drowned.... Then the people came out to see what had happened, and when they came to Jesus, they found the man from whom the demons had gone sitting at the feet of Jesus, clothed and in his right mind. And they were afraid.

~Luke 8:30-33, 35

It was the Legion
not the swine
they feared.
And now—
a man
in his right mind.
The Romans watch
No wonder they are afraid.

Monday

Now the word of the LORD came to Jonah son of Amittai, saying, "Go at once to Nineveh, that great city, and cry out against it; for their wickedness has come up before me." But Jonah set out to flee to Tarshish from the presence of the LORD.
~Jonah 1:1-3a

Am I fleeing
from a Nineveh
today?
Where or what
is a Tarshish
in my life?

"Wherever they do not welcome you, as you are leaving the town shake the dust off your feet as a testimony against them."
~Luke 9:5

Dust of
memories
cling to my heart
though I have shaken out
the last grains of hope.

Wednesday

Then the LORD said [to Jonah], "You are concerned about the bush, for which you did not labor and which you did not grow; it came into being in a night and perished in a night. And should I not be concerned about Nineveh, that great city, in which there are more than a hundred and twenty thousand persons who do not know their right hand from their left, and also many animals?"
~Jonah 4:10-11

It is easier
to care for a plant
than all those
Ninevites
in the world
who don't know their right hand from their left!!!

Thursday

Paul had gathered a bundle of brushwood and was putting it on the fire, when a viper, driven out by the heat, fastened itself on his hand. When the natives saw the creature hanging from his hand, they said to one another, "This man must be a murderer; though he has escaped from the sea, justice has not allowed him to live." He, however, shook off the creature into the fire and suffered no harm. They were expecting him to swell up or drop dead, but after they had waited a long time and saw that nothing unusual had happened to him, they changed their minds and began to say he was a god.
~Acts 28:3-6

Winds
gust and storm
switching directions
from one moment to the next.
Blowing
the un-centered
off course.

Friday

Some put their trust in chariots and some in horses,
    but we will call upon the Name of the
    LORD our God.
~Psalm 20:7

Some put their trust in stealth bombers
and some in poison gas
but in the end we will all be dead
and answer for our choices.
Waging war is easy
but waging peace is true victory.

Saturday

Let the faithful rejoice in triumph;
    let them be joyful on their beds.
~Psalm 149:5

Waking or sleeping
Dreaming of joy.

Do not be ashamed to confess your sins,
    and do not try to stop the current of a river.
Do not subject yourself to a fool,
    or show partiality to a ruler.
~Ecclesiasticus 4:26-27

Like iron filings
fools line up
in the magnetic force fields
of power.

Monday

Faithful friends are a sturdy shelter:
 whoever finds one has found a treasure.
Faithful friends are beyond price;
 no amount can balance their worth.
Faithful friends are life-saving medicine;
 and those who fear the Lord will find them.
~Ecclesiasticus 6:14-16

Friendships build
heart homes
where we can be made whole.

Tuesday

"Which of these three, do you think, was a neighbor to the man who fell into the hands of robbers?" He said, "The one who showed him mercy." Jesus said to him, "Go and do likewise."
~Luke 10:36-37

Battered and bruised
in the ditches of life
looking up into the faces
of strangers and friends
the alien and the familiar
who will show mercy?

Wednesday

Sovereignty passes from nation to nation
    on account of injustice and insolence and wealth.
How can dust and ashes be proud?
    Even in life the human body decays.
A long illness baffles the physician;
    the king of today will die tomorrow.
For when one is dead
    he inherits maggots and vermin and worms.
~Ecclesiasticus 10:8-11

What will be our legacy
dust and ashes?
justice and compassion?

Thursday

Now as they went on their way, Jesus entered a certain village, where a woman named Martha welcomed him into her home. She had a sister named Mary, who sat at the LORD's feet and listened to what he was saying. But Martha was distracted by her many tasks; so she came to him and asked, "Jesus, do you not care that my sister has left me to do all the work by myself? Tell her then to help me." But he answered her, "Martha, Martha, you are worried and distracted by many things; there is need of only one thing. Mary has chosen the better part, which will not be taken away from her."
~Luke 10:38-42

Dishes always need to be done
Laundry awaits the washing
Dust piles up on the windowsills
Day after day.

Moments with friends flee by
and may not come again.

Friday

Before each person are life and death,
    and whichever one chooses will be given.
~Ecclesiasticus 15:17

Lifegiving.
Deathdealing.
For me?
For those I love?
For the world?
Sometimes
it is not clear
which choice
is which.

Saturday

"For where two or three are gathered in my name, I am there among them."
~Matthew 18:20

Not out there
somewhere,
but here
in the spaces
between us,
gathered.

"When the unclean spirit has gone out of a person, it wanders through waterless regions looking for a resting place, but not finding any, it says, 'I will return to my house from which I came.' When it comes, it finds it swept and put in order. Then it goes and brings seven other spirits more evil than itself, and they enter and live there; and the last state of that person is worse than the first."
~Luke 11:24-26

Swept and orderly
empty and waiting
Maybe a little mess is a good thing?

Monday

While he was saying this, a woman in the crowd raised her voice and said to him, "Blessed is the womb that bore you and the breasts that nursed you!" But he said, "Blessed rather are those who hear the word of God and obey it!"
~Luke 11:27-28

Like mother's milk
for infant bodies
Avoid colic of the spirit—
Take in the Word
for growing souls.

Tuesday

While [Jesus] was speaking, a Pharisee invited him to dine with him; so he went in and took his place at the table. The Pharisee was amazed to see that he did not first wash before dinner. Then the LORD said to him, "Now you Pharisees clean the outside of the cup and of the dish, but inside you are full of greed and wickedness.... For you tithe mint and rue and herbs of all kinds, and neglect justice and love of God."
~Luke 11:37-39, 42

Inviting Jesus to dinner
is risky business.
One may be served
unanticipated desserts!

Wednesday

The LORD, the God of gods, has spoken;
　　he has called the earth from the rising of the sun
　　　　to its setting.
Out of Zion, perfect in its beauty,
　　God reveals himself in glory.
~Psalm 50:1-2

Earth turns with a Word
An eternal round dance
Sun and stars and moons
Dance the days away

Thursday

Like one who kills a son before his father's eyes
  is the person who offers a sacrifice
    from the property of the poor.
The bread of the needy is the life of the poor;
  whoever deprives them of it is a murderer.
To take away a neighbor's living
    is to commit murder;
  to deprive an employee of wages is to shed blood.
~Ecclesiasticus 34:24-27

Many ways to be a murderer
without taking out gun or knife.

Friday

"Do not be afraid, little flock, for it is your Father's good pleasure to give you the kingdom. Sell your possessions, and give alms. Make purses for yourselves that do not wear out, an unfailing treasure in heaven, where no thief comes near and no moth destroys. For where your treasure is, there your heart will be also."
~Luke 12:32-34

Purses fashioned
with the fabric of life
Contain only the essentials
for the Journey.

Saturday

If I speak in the tongues of mortals and of angels, but do not have love, I am a noisy gong or a clanging cymbal. And if I have prophetic powers, and understand all mysteries and all knowledge, and if I have all faith, so as to remove mountains, but do not have love, I am nothing.

~1 Corinthians 13:1-2

Nothing
Zero
Empty circle
Surrounded by a ring of noise.
Only Love can fill the hole inside.

Proper 26: Sunday
Week of the Sunday closest to November 2

All these rely on their hands,
    and all are skillful in their own work.
Without them no city can be inhabited,
    and wherever they live, they will not go hungry.
Yet they are not sought out for the council
        of the people,
    nor do they attain eminence in
        the public assembly.
They do not sit in the judge's seat,
    nor do they understand the decisions of the courts;
they cannot expound discipline or judgment,
    and they are not found among the rulers.
But they maintain the fabric of the world,
    and their concern is for the exercise of their trade.
How different the one who devotes himself
    to the study of the law of the Most High!
~Ecclesiasticus 38:31-34

When the fabric is frayed
we need more needleworkers.

Then he told this parable: "A man had a fig tree planted in his vineyard; and he came looking for fruit on it and found none. So he said to the gardener, 'See here! For three years I have come looking for fruit on this fig tree, and still I find none. Cut it down! Why should it be wasting the soil?' He replied, 'Sir, let it alone for one more year, until I dig around it and put manure on it. If it bears fruit next year, well and good; but if not, you can cut it down.'"

~Luke 13:6-9

Trees taking up space
in the garden
hope for the gardener
to encourage growth.
Tree or Tender?
Which am I today?

Tuesday

But the LORD answered him, and said, "You hypocrites! Does not each of you on the sabbath untie his ox or his donkey from the manger, and lead it away to give it water? And ought not this woman, a daughter of Abraham who Satan bound for eighteen long years, be set free from this bondage on the sabbath day?"
~Luke 13:15-16

weight of years
burdens of life
pain, thirst
longing, aching, seeking
streams of water
washing away the chains
dancing, laughing, singing.

And I saw three foul spirits like frogs coming from the mouth of the dragon, from the mouth of the beast, and from the mouth of the false prophet.
~Revelation 16:13

Words leap out
from the heart of hate.
Flames devouring truth.

Thursday

And now bless the God of all,
    who everywhere works great wonders,
who fosters our growth from birth,
    and deals with us according to his mercy.
May he give us gladness of heart,
    and may there be peace in our days
    in Israel, as in the days of old.
~Ecclesiasticus 50:22-23

The cry for peace
screams in the silence
of dying children.

Friday

"But when you are invited, go and sit down at the lowest place, so that when your host comes, he may say to you, 'Friend, move up higher'; then you will be honored in the presence of all who sit at the table with you."
~Luke 14:10

All are close to the Center
when the table is round.

Saturday

While I was still young, before I went on my travels,
    I sought wisdom openly in my prayer.
Before the temple I asked for her,
    and I will search for her until the end.
~Ecclesiasticus 51:13-14

Wisdom:
Compass and sextant
through fog banks
of life.
The original
Global Positioning System!

Proper 27: Sunday
Week of the Sunday closest to November 9

"But when you give a banquet, invite the poor, the crippled, the lame, and the blind. And you will be blessed, because they cannot repay you, for you will be repaid the resurrection of the righteous."
~Luke 14:13-14

Frayed and torn
tattered lives.
are the cloth of gold
for the Banquet.

Monday

Then I fell down at his feet to worship him, but he said to me, "You must not do that! I am a fellow servant with you and your comrades who hold the testimony of Jesus. Worship God!"
~Revelation 19:10

The playing field is level
and all are players
on the team
in this game.

"Or what woman having ten silver coins, if she loses one of them, does not light a lamp, sweep the house, and search carefully until she finds it? When she has found it, she calls together her friends and neighbors, saying, 'Rejoice with me, for I have found the coin that I had lost.' Just so, I tell you, there is joy in the presence of the angels of God over one sinner who repents."
~Luke 15:8-10

Sweeping and searching
to find all the fallen coins
Cleaning lady God
sharp eyed
spies even
the least cent.

Wednesday

"So he set off and went to his father. But while he was still far off, his father saw him and was filled with compassion; he ran and put his arms around him and kissed him."
~Luke 15:20

Shame
transformed
by a kiss.

Thursday

Afterward
> I will pour out my spirit on all flesh;
> your sons and your daughters shall prophesy,
> your old men shall dream dreams,
> and your youth shall see visions.
~Joel 2:28

Stars and comets
streaking through
hearts and minds
birthing worlds
of dreams and visions.

Friday

The LORD will record as he enrolls the peoples,
"These also were born there."
The singers and the dancers will say,
"All my fresh springs are in you."
~Psalm 87:5-6

Source of being
Breathing us out into the world
and inspiring us to return.

Saturday

"Woe to you, scribes, and Pharisees, hypocrites! For you tithe mint, dill, and cumin, and have neglected the weightier matters of the law: justice and mercy and faith."
~Matthew 23:23

Mint, cumin, and dill
cannot dispel
the bitter taste of exploitation.

Proper 28: Sunday
Week of the Sunday closest to November 16

What good is it, my brothers and sisters, if you say you have faith but do not have works? Can faith save you? If a brother or sister is naked and lacks daily food, and one of you says to them, "Go in peace; keep warm and eat your fill," and yet you do not supply their bodily needs, what is the good of that? So faith by itself, if it has no works, is dead.

But someone will say, "You have faith and I have works." Show me your faith apart from your works, and I by my works will show you my faith.
~James 2:14-18

Faith is illusion
without substance.

From the same mouth come blessing and cursing. My brothers and sisters, this ought not to be so. Does a spring pour forth from the same opening both fresh and brackish water? Can a fig tree, my brothers and sisters, yield olives, or a grapevine figs? No more can salt water yield fresh.
~James 3:10-12

Figs, olives, and grapes
Fruit of vine and tree
Roots seeking the Water of Life.

Tuesday

Then Jesus asked, "Were not ten made clean? But the other nine, where are they? Was none of them found to return and give praise to God except this foreigner?" Then he said to him, "Get up and go on your way; your faith has made you well."
~Luke 17:17-19

I would have thanked you but:
1. my dinner was burning
2. my kids were crying
3. my business needed me
4. I didn't have any note cards
5. I didn't want to embarrass you
6. I thought you knew
7. I was tired
8. I was so excited
9. I forgot.

Wednesday

Once Jesus was asked by the Pharisees when the kingdom of God was coming, and he answered, "The kingdom of God is not coming with things that can be observed; nor will they say, 'Look, here it is!' or 'There it is!' For, in fact, the kingdom of God is among you."
~Luke 17:20-21

The Holy One
dwelling
in the spaces
between hands
and arms
and hearts
reaching out
to welcome.

Thursday

Then Jesus told them a parable about their need to pray always and not to lose heart.
~Luke 18:1

Prayer
exercises
the heart.

But for you who revere my name the sun of righteousness shall rise, with healing in its wings. You shall go out leaping like calves from the stall.
~Malachi 4:2

Spiritual paths
invite dancing.

Saturday

He said to them, "It is written,
'My house shall be called a house of prayer';
but you are making it a den of robbers."
~Matthew 21:13

Sneaking in
to snatch
the gifts
Thieves of
the treasury
of heaven
steal from themselves.

Proper 29: Sunday
Week of the Sunday closest to November 23

"Indeed, it is easier for a camel to go through the eye of a needle than for someone who is rich to enter the kingdom of God."
~Luke 18:25

saddlebags
strip from sides
of bruised humps
of greed
It will take more
than a diet to get ready for this feast.

Monday

As the eyes of servants look to the hand
      of their masters,
  and the eyes of a maid to the hand of her mistress,
So our eyes look to the LORD our God,
  until he show us his mercy.
~Psalm 123:2-3

Hand of God
left or right
old and gnarled
young and plump
pampered and painted
scarred and wounded
open palm or closed fist?

Tuesday

All who saw it began to grumble and said, "He has gone to be the guest of one who is a sinner."
~Luke 19:7

When will we be host
to the Guest?

Wednesday

Let your priests be clothed with righteousness;
     let your faithful people sing with joy.
~Psalm 132:9

Garments from God
outshine designer duds.

Some of the Pharisees in the crowd said to him, "Teacher, order your disciples to stop." He answered, "I tell you, if these were silent, the stones would shout out."
~Luke 19:39-40

Shouting stones
break the silence
Pebbles proclaim
even the sand speaks
When the Holy One appears.

Friday

As Jesus came near and saw the city, he wept over it, saying, "If you, even you, had only recognized on this day the things that make for peace!"
~Luke 19:41-42

Can heaven's weeping
be heard over the drums of war?

Saturday

Appendix: List of Citations Used

Week 1 of Advent
Sunday: 1 Thessalonians 5:1-11
Monday: 2 Peter 1:1-11
Tuesday: 2 Peter 1:12-21
Wednesday: Matthew 21:23-32
Thursday: 2 Peter 3:11-18
Friday: Psalm 16
Saturday: Psalm 116

Week 2 of Advent
Sunday: Psalm 30
Monday: Revelation 1:1-8
Tuesday: Amos 7:10-17,24-25
Wednesday: Matthew 23:1-12
Thursday: Matthew 23:13-26
Friday: Revelation 2:18-29
Saturday: Revelation 3:1-6

Week 3 of Advent
Sunday: John 5:30-47
Monday: Psalm 41
Tuesday: Revelation 3:14-22.
Wednesday: Psalm 119:49-72
Thursday: Matthew 25:1-13
Friday: Zechariah 7:8-8:8
Saturday: Matthew 25:31-46

Week 4 of Advent
Sunday: John 3:16-21
Monday: Luke 1:1-25
Tuesday: 1 Samuel 2:1b-10
Wednesday: Luke 1:39-56
Thursday: Luke 1:57-66
Friday: Matthew 1:1-17
December 24: Revelation 21:22-22:5
Christmas Eve: Matthew 1:18-25

Christmas Day and Following
Christmas Day: Micah 4:1-5, 5:2-4
First Sunday after Christmas: Luke 2:22-
Dec 28 Holy Innocents: Collect of the Day, BCP
Dec 29 Matthew 2:13-18
Dec 30: 3 John 1-15
Dec 31: John 5:1-15
Holy Name: Isaiah 62:1-5,10-12

Second Sunday after Christmas
Sunday: Wisdom 7:3-14
Jan 2: 1 Kings 19:1-8
Jan 3: 1 Kings 19:9-18
Jan 4: Ephesians 5:1-20
Jan 5: Jonah 2:2-9

Eve of Epiphany: John 15:1-11
The Epiphany and Following
Epiphany: Isaiah 49:1
Jan 7: Colossians 1:1-14
Jan 8: John 7:37-52
Jan 9: John 8:12-19

Jan 10: Genesis 2:7, John 10:7-17
Jan 11: Isaiah 55: 3-9
Jan 12: John 15:1-16
Eve of 1 Epiphany: Ephesians 4:1-16

Week of 1 Epiphany
Sunday: John 5: 1-15
Monday: John 1:1-18
Tuesday: Mark 1:29-45
Wednesday: Hebrews 2:11-18
Thursday: John 1:43-51
Friday: Hebrews 3:12-19
Saturday: Hebrews 4:1-13

Week of 2 Epiphany
Sunday: Ephesians 4:1-16
Monday: John 2:23-3:15
Tuesday: Genesis 9:1-17
Wednesday: Hebrews 6:1-12
Thursday: John 4:1-15
Friday: Genesis 11:27-12:8
Saturday: John 4:27-42

Week of 3 Epiphany
Sunday: Mark 7:31-37
Monday: Hebrews 8:1-13
Tuesday: John 5:1-18
Wednesday: Psalm 119:49-72
Thursday: Psalm 50
Friday: John 6:1-15
Saturday: Hebrews 10:26-39

Week of 4 Epiphany

Sunday: Genesis 18:16-33
Monday: Genesis 19:1-29
Tuesday: Genesis 21:1-21
Wednesday: Hebrews 11:23-31
Thursday: Hebrews 11:32-12:2
Friday: John 7:1-13
Saturday: Hebrews 12:12-29

Week of 5 Epiphany

Sunday: Mark 10:13-22
Monday: Hebrews 13:1-16
Tuesday: John 7:53-8:11
Wednesday: Romans 12:1-8
Thursday: Romans 12:9-21
Friday: Genesis 27:46-28:4,10-22
Saturday: Romans 14:1-23

Week of 6 Epiphany

Sunday: 1 Timothy 3:14-4:10
Monday: 1 John 1:1-10
Tuesday: John 9:18-41
Wednesday: John 10:1-18
Thursday: John 10:19-30
Friday: Genesis 32:22-33:17
Saturday: John 11:1-16

Week of 7 Epiphany

Sunday: Mark 10:35-45
Monday: Proverbs 3:11-20
Tuesday: Proverbs 4:1-27

Wednesday: John 11:45-54
Thursday: 1 John 5:13-21
Friday: Proverbs 8:1-21
Saturday: 2 Timothy 1:1-14

Week of 8 Epiphany
Sunday: Proverbs 9:1-12
Monday: Proverbs 10:1-12
Tuesday: Proverbs 15:16-33
Wednesday: John 13:1-20
Thursday: Timothy 4:1-8
Friday: Timothy 4:9-22 and John 13:31-38
Saturday: Proverbs 25:15-28

Week of Last Epiphany
Sunday: Luke 9:18-27
Monday: John 18:15-18, 25-27
Tuesday: John 18:28-38
Ash Wednesday: Amos 5:6-15
Thursday: Psalm 37
Friday: Philippians 4:1-9
Saturday: Philippians 4:10-20

Week of 1 Lent
Sunday: John 12:44-50
Monday: Mark 1:1-13
Tuesday: Genesis 37:12-24
Wednesday: Mark 1:29-45
Thursday: Mark 2:1-12
Friday: Mark 2:13-22
Saturday: Psalm 139

Week of 2 Lent

Sunday: Genesis 41:14-45
Monday: Mark 3:7-19a
Tuesday: Mark 3:19b-35
Wednesday: Mark 4:1-20
Thursday: 1 Corinthians 6:12-30
Friday: Mark 4:35-41
Saturday: Mark 5:1-20

Week of 3 Lent

Sunday: Genesis 44:1-7
Monday: Mark 5:21-43
Tuesday: Mark 6:1-13
Wednesday: 1 Corinthians 8:1-13
Thursday: Mark 6:30-46
Friday: 1 Corinthians 9:16-27
Saturday: Psalm 90

Week of 4 Lent

Sunday: Romans 8:11-25
Monday: Genesis 49:1-28
Tuesday: Genesis 49:29-50:14
Wednesday: Mark 8:11-26
Thursday: Exodus 1:6-22
Friday: 1 Corinthians 12:27-13:3
Saturday: Mark 9:14-29

Week of 5 Lent

Sunday: Romans 12:1-21
Monday: 1 Corinthians 14:1-19
Tuesday: Exodus 5:1-6:1
Wednesday: Mark 10:1-16

Thursday: Psalm 142
Friday: Mark 10:32-45
Saturday: 2 Corinthians 4:13-18

Holy Week
Palm Sunday: Luke 19:41-48
Monday: 2 Corinthians 1:1-7
Tuesday: 2 Corinthians 1:8-22
Wednesday: Mark 12:1-11
Maundy Thursday: 1 Corinthians 10:14-17, 11:27-32
Good Friday: Lamentations 3:1-9, 19-33
Holy Saturday: Lamentations 3:37-58

Easter Week
Easter Day: Luke 24:13-35
Monday: Exodus 12:14-27
Tuesday: 1 Corinthians 15:12-28
Wednesday: Matthew 28:1-16
Thursday: Matthew 28:16-20
Friday: Luke 24:1-12
Saturday: Matthew 24:43-44

Week of 2 Easter
Sunday: Exodus 14:5-22
Monday: John 14:1-17
Tuesday: Exodus 15:1-21
Wednesday: 1 Peter 2:1-10
Thursday: 1 Peter 2:11-25
Friday: John 16:1-15
Saturday: John 16:16-33

Week of 3 Easter
Sunday: Mark 16:9-20
Monday: Psalm 15
Tuesday: Matthew 3:7-12
Wednesday: Matthew 3:13-17
Thursday: Psalm 37:19-42
Friday: Colossians 2:8-23
Saturday: Matthew 4:18-25

Week of 4 Easter
Sunday: Mark 6:30-44
Monday: Exodus 32:1-20
Tuesday: Psalm 103
Wednesday: Exodus 33:1-23
Thursday: Matthew 5:21-26
Friday: Matthew 5:27-37
Saturday: Matthew 5:38-48

Week of 5 Easter
Sunday: Luke 4:16-30
Monday: Psalm 56
Tuesday: Matthew 6:7-15
Wednesday: Leviticus 19:1-18
Thursday: Matthew 6:25-34
Friday: Matthew 7:1-12
Saturday: Matthew 7:13-21

Week of 6 Easter
Sunday: Luke 12:13-21
Monday: Psalm 80
Tuesday: Leviticus 26:1-20
Eve of Ascension: 2 Kings 2:1-15

Ascension Day: Hebrews 2:5-18 and Matthew 28:16-20
Friday: 1 Samuel 2:1-10
Saturday: Ephesians 2:11-22

Week of 7 Easter
Sunday: Exodus 3:1-12
Monday: Psalm 89:1-18
Tuesday: 1 Samuel 16:1-13a
Wednesday: Ephesians 4:1-16
Thursday: Ephesians 4:17-32
Friday: Jeremiah 31:27-34
Saturday: Ezekiel 36:22-27
Eve of Pentecost: Exodus 19:3-8a, 16-20

Proper 1 (Week of the Sunday closest to May 11)
Day of Pentecost: John 4:19-26
Monday: Zechariah 2:1-13
Tuesday: Psalm 106:1-18
Wednesday: 1 John 2:12-17
Thursday: Matthew 10:16-23
Friday: Matthew 10:24-33
Saturday: Matthew 10:34-42

Proper 2 (Week of the Sunday closest to May 18)
Trinity Sunday: Job 38:1-11; 42:1-5
Monday: Proverbs 3:13-20
Tuesday: John 4:7-21
Wednesday: Matthew 11:2-15
Thursday: Genesis 40:5-8
Friday: Psalm 16
Saturday: Isaiah 28:20

Proper 3 (Week of the Sunday closest to May 25)
Sunday: Psalm 148
Monday: Psalm 25
Tuesday: Psalm 18
Wednesday: Isaiah 1:1-18
Thursday: Psalm 37:1-18
Friday: Psalm 31
Saturday: Mark 3:32-35

Proper 4 (Week of the Sunday closest to June 1)
Sunday: Mark 2:1-12
Monday: Psalm 41
Tuesday: Hebrews 11:24-25
Wednesday: John 5:39-40,42
Thursday: Isaiah 8:21b-9:1
Friday: Isaiah 10:1-4
Saturday: Luke 22:31-33

Proper 5 (Week of the Sunday closest to June 8)
Sunday: Ecclesiastes 6:1-12 and Luke 12:32-40
Monday: Matthew 7:1-12
Tuesday: Ecclesiastes 8:14-9:10
Wednesday: Galatians 5:1-15
Thursday: Ecclesiastes 11:1-8
Friday: Psalm 69:1-38
Saturday: Psalm 23

Proper 6 (Week of the Sunday closest to June 15)
Sunday: Psalm 31
Monday: Romans 1:1-15
Tuesday: Numbers 11:1-23
Wednesday: Matthew 18:1-9

Thursday: Numbers 12:1-16
Friday: Matthew 18:21-35
Saturday: Psalm 87

Proper 7 (Week of the Sunday closest to June 22)
Sunday: Luke 12:49-56
Monday: Matthew 19:13-22
Tuesday: Matthew 19:23-30
Wednesday: Matthew 20:1-16
Thursday: Isaiah 52:7-12
Friday: Matthew 20:29-34
Saturday: Romans 6:1-11

Proper 8 (Week of the Sunday closest to June 29)
Sunday: Luke 13:10-17
Monday: Numbers 22:1-21
Tuesday: Romans 7:1-12
Wednesday: Matthew 21:33-46
Thursday: Psalm 131
Friday: Psalm 140
Saturday: Psalm 137

Proper 9 (Week of the Sunday closest to July 6)
Sunday: Psalm 112
Monday: Psalm 1
Tuesday: Psalm 5
Wednesday: Deuteronomy 1:1-18
Thursday: 1 Peter 3:13-4:6
Friday: Psalm 16
Saturday: Psalm 20

Proper 10 (Week of the Sunday closest to July 13)
Sunday: Joshua 1:1-18
Monday: Joshua 2:1-14
Tuesday: Matthew 25:14-30
Wednesday: Romans 11:25-36
Thursday: Romans 12:1-8
Friday: Romans 12: 9- 21
Saturday: Matthew 26:26-35

Proper 11 (Week of the Sunday closest to July 20)
Sunday: Revelations 21:22-22:5
Monday: Matthew 26:36-46
Tuesday: Romans 14: 1-12
Wednesday: Matthew 26:57-68
Thursday: Psalm 50
Friday: Matthew 27:1-10
Saturday: Psalm 55

Proper 12 (Week of the Sunday closest to July 27)
Sunday: Acts 28:23-31
Monday: Joshua 24:16-33
Tuesday: Matthew 27:32-44
Wednesday: Matthew 27:45-54
Thursday: Matthew 27:55-66
Friday: Acts 2:1-21
Saturday: Revelation 22:6-13

Proper 13 (Week of the Sunday closest to August 3)
Sunday: Mark 3:20-30
Monday: Judges 6:25-40
Tuesday: John 1:19-28
Wednesday: John 1:29-42

Thursday: Psalm 145
Friday: John 2:1-12
Saturday: John 2:13-25

Proper 14 (Week of the Sunday closest to August 10)
Sunday: Judges 11:1-11,29-40
Monday: Psalm 89:1-18
Tuesday: Acts 5:27-42
Wednesday: Matthew 16:21-28
Thursday: Psalm 105:1-22
Friday: Nehemiah 7:73b-8:3,5-18
Saturday: John 5:1-18

Proper 15 (Week of the Sunday closest to August 17)
Sunday: Matthew 13:31-35
Monday: Reading: Luke 12:22-31
Tuesday: Psalm 122
Wednesday: Matthew 13:53-58
Thursday: Psalm 57
Friday: Reading: Psalm 61
Saturday: Reading: Psalm 69

Proper 16 (Week of the Sunday closest to August 24)
Sunday: Matthew 9:18-26
Monday: Matthew 11:7-15
Tuesday: Matthew 11:16-24
Wednesday: 1 Corinthians 15:51-58
Thursday: Luke 10:25-37
Friday: Job 9:1-15,32-35
Saturday: Job 9:1, 10:1-9, 16-22

Proper 17 (Week of the Sunday closest to August 31)
Sunday: Psalm 114
Monday: Acts11:19-30
Tuesday: Job 12:1,13:3-17,21-27
Wednesday: Psalm 119:25-48
Thursday: John 9:1-17
Friday: John 9:18-41
Saturday: John 10:1-18

Proper 18 (Week of the Sunday closest to September 7)
Sunday: Matthew 5:13-20
Monday: John 10:19-30
Tuesday: Acts 14:1-18
Wednesday: John 11:1-16
Thursday: John 11:17-29
Friday: John 11:30-44
Saturday: Psalm 55

Proper 19 (Week of the Sunday closest to September 14)
Sunday: Matthew 5:21-26
Monday: Acts 15:36-16:5
Tuesday: Acts16:6-15
Wednesday: Job 42:1-17
Thursday: Psalm 74
Friday: John 12:36b-43
Saturday: Acts 17:16-34

Proper 20 (Week of the Sunday closest to September 21)
Sunday: Psalm 93

Monday: Psalm 80
Tuesday: Esther 5:1-14
Wednesday: Luke 4:1-13
Thursday: Psalm 85
Friday: Luke 4:31- 37
Saturday: Luke 4:38-44

Proper 21 (Week of the Sunday closest to September 28)
Sunday: James 3:1-13
Monday: Acts 20:17-38
Tuesday: Luke 5:12-26
Wednesday: Hosea 4:11-19
Thursday: Luke 6:6-11
Friday: Luke 6:12-26
Saturday: Luke 6:27-38

Proper 22 (Week of the Sunday closest to October 5)
Sunday: Micah 1:1-9
Monday: Psalm 106:1-48
Tuesday: Acts 23:12-24
Wednesday: Micah 2:1-13 and Psalm 119:145-176
Thursday: Acts 24:1-23
Friday: Micah 3:9-4:5
Saturday: Luke 8:16-25

Proper 23 (Week of the Sunday closest to October 12)
Sunday: Micah 6:1-8
Monday: Luke 8:26-39
Tuesday: Jonah 1:1-17a
Wednesday: Luke 9:1-17
Thursday: Jonah 3:1-4:11

Friday: Acts 28:1-16
Saturday: Psalm 20

Proper 24 (Week of the Sunday closest to October 19)
Sunday: Psalm 149
Monday: Ecclesiasticus 4:20-5:7
Tuesday: Ecclesiasticus 6:5-17
Wednesday: Luke 10:17-24 [36-37]
Thursday: Ecclesiasticus 10:1-18
Friday: Luke 10:38-42
Saturday: Ecclesiasticus 15:9-20

Proper 25 (Week of the Sunday closest to October 26)
Sunday: Matthew 18:15-20
Monday: Luke 11:14-26
Tuesday: Luke 11:27-36
Wednesday: Luke 11:37-52
Thursday: Psalm 50
Friday: Ecclesiasticus 34:1-8, 18-22
Saturday: Luke 12:32-48

Proper 26 (Week of the Sunday closest to November 2)
Sunday: 1 Corinthians 12:27-13:13
Monday: Ecclesiasticus 38:24-34
Tuesday: Luke 13:1-9
Wednesday: Luke 13:10-17
Thursday: Revelation 16:12-21
Friday: Ecclesiasticus 50:1, 11-24
Saturday: Luke 14:1-11

Proper 27 (Week of the Sunday closest to November 9)
Sunday: Ecclesiasticus 51:13-22
Monday: Luke 14:12-24
Tuesday: Revelation 19:1-10
Wednesday: Luke 15:1-10
Thursday: Luke 15:1-2,11-32
Friday: Joel 2:28-3:8
Saturday: Psalm 87

Proper 28 (Week of the Sunday closest to November 16)
Sunday: Matthew 23:13-24
Monday: James 2:14-26
Tuesday: James 3:1-12
Wednesday: Luke 17:11-19
Thursday: Luke 17:20-37
Friday: Luke 18:1-8
Saturday: Malachi 3:13-4:6

Proper 29 (Week of the Sunday closest to November 23)
Sunday: Matthew 21:1-13
Monday: Luke 18:15-30
Tuesday: Psalm 123
Wednesday: Luke 19:1-10
Thursday: Psalm 132
Friday: Luke 19:28-40
Saturday: Luke 19:41-48

About the Author

Ann Fontaine lives and works in Wyoming as an Episcopal priest. Before attending Harvard Divinity School and graduating with a Masters of Divinity, she worked in education and training, traveling for the church to lead workshops and serving as member of various boards and committees. January 6, 1996, on the Feast of the Epiphany, she was ordained to the priesthood. Her vocation as a priest is to serve as an interim priest to congregations who are exploring new ways to see themselves as a community and who are developing new models of leadership. As a result, she has traveled widely throughout her home state of Wyoming. The long drives through open country and high mountain passes have given her time for reflection. In 1998 she began writing responses to the readings set out in the Daily Office of the Episcopal Church's Book of Common Prayer. She shared these daily meditations with friends and family who encouraged her to gather them together into this book.

This book would not exist without the advice and long hours of editing by our daughter, Kristin Fontaine. Many thanks to her and my family, friends and readers of Dailyoffice@yahoogroups.com